D1329603

A Place Called Sweet Apple

Country Living and Southern Recipes

CELESTINE SIBLEY

Illustrations by Scarlett B. Rickenbaker

Peachtree Publishers, Ltd.

Published by
PEACHTREE PUBLISHERS, LTD.
494 Armour Circle, NE
Atlanta, Georgia 30324

Manufactured in the United States of America

Second printing

ISBN: 0-931948-72-X

For Jack Strong
without whose help
it would have been impossible.

Contents

Prologue

The sin of pride was upon me. In the early morning light Sweet Apple cabin looked charming to me. The sun struck the white oak boards of the roof just right to bring out the weathered silver in them. The log walls were a soft gray-green with moss and the world around us was shot through with red and gold where the light hit a dogwood, a maple or a sweetgum tree.

I felt good and pleased that after all these months of living in the country I had gone to the trouble of getting our old-time, once-a-week cleaning woman to come out from town and give the cabin a going-over for company.

My son took the truck and went into Sandy Springs twelve miles away to meet her at the bus stop. She stepped out of the truck, wearing her new camouflage-colored hunting hat and carrying the ubiquitous canvas zipper bag I have never seen her without.

"Lord have mercy!" she cried when her eyes fell on the cabin. "Is we here? Is this where you live now? Oh Lord, Lord, ain't that a shame?"

"Look at the pretty logs," I entreated.

"Humph!" she snorted. "I bet they is full of snakes."

The interior was even more appalling to her.

"To think, to *think*," she cried, "that you have come to this! A nice lady like you living all them years in that big old house on Thirteenth Street—and you down to this. Oh Lord, I wish I hadn't come to this place to see this thing! It's pitiful, pitiful."

All the time she talked she was taking off her coat, finding a safe place for her zipper bag and glaring at everything from beneath the brim of her hunting hat.

"Hush, now," I said. "I don't want to hear another word against my new home. I like it. Lots of folks like it, even rich folks who live in fine three-story mansions."

She laughed derisively, going "Hoo . . . hoo . . . hoo." But she didn't say anything more to me for a long time. She talked to herself, chanting like a litany the names of her "other ladies" who live in nice city homes—some of them brick.

I heard her call the name of the Monday lady and the Tuesday lady and the one who succeeded me as the Wednesday lady. Finally, incensed, I interrupted meanly.

"Isn't she the one who likes plastic everything?"

"She a nice lady, she got a beautiful home," she replied with dignity.

"Oh," I said and took my coffee and went out in the back yard to pout.

Work has ever been a consolation to her. She's always been refreshed and challenged by a dirty stove or a grimy bathtub. She worked quietly for a time but once I heard her talking out the window in my direction, her remarks ostensibly addressed to the Almighty.

"God, You want your chil'ren to live good, I know You do. *She* a child of God, how come she is *so* afflicted?"

This conversation and the pleasure of getting all the grease off the oven must have done her good because when she finished and I drove her back to the bus stop she said she might come back again if I ever needed her.

"I ain't go' say nothing against your house," she promised. "Peoples ask me about it, I just say, 'It suits *her*.'"

An interesting old cabin

How an old abandoned house can take hold of a reasonably sane woman's heart, fill her mind, lap up her energy and change her life is still something of a mystery to me. I was a content city dweller when I first saw Sweet Apple cabin. I had lived for more than fifteen years within walking distance of Atlanta's Five Points and had been smug about the fact that I reared my children without putting in long hours chauffeuring them to school, the Brownies, the library, dancing class or the piano teacher. They could walk or ride the bus everywhere they had to go. When we needed a taste of country living we had a little two-room shack a hundred miles away on Holly Creek in the mountains of north Georgia.

Then one day in the spring of 1961 I rode out in the country with our friend Jack Strong to look at land. Someone had told him to look up W. H. Smellie, a long-time Atlanta physiotherapist who had moved to the northern part of the county and launched a real estate business.

"Doc," as we were soon to learn hundreds of people called him, said he had just the tract to interest Jack—twenty acres of woodland with a good hilltop building site, a view of mountains and a stream big enough to make a sizable lake.

"On the way, let me show you an interesting old cabin," Doc said. "It's not for sale but I think you'd like to see it."

We were later to learn that Doc is an inveterate "on-the-wayer." On any kind of trip to anywhere he can think of some side point of interest—view, house, barn, road or person —that you ought not to miss.

That day he took us down a dirt road a city block or so off the pavement and parked on the edge of a wild plum thicket. The only sign of habitation was a rusty tin roof barely visible beyond the plum trees and a tangle of dead fruit trees supporting a lush, jungle-like growth of honeysuckle.

"It's too rough to try to get in the front door," Doc said, "but there used to be a path to the back."

He led the way along a faint path, pulling back thorny swatches of blackberry to let us pass and ducking under tree branches that crowded close. The back door stood ajar and to reach it we had to climb over the bleached and decayed carcass of the collapsed shedroom which had once served as a kitchen.

Doc murmured something about its being a good place for snakes but he doubted if there were any out so early.

We stepped gingerly over rotten sills and brittle fragments of wooden shingles into the main room—a long room whose walls were halved logs fifteen inches or more wide with hand-planed boards covering the cracks in between. It had a rock fireplace taking up most of one end of the room with a crooked little window next to it, another lopsided window at the other end and a ladder leading to a loftroom.

Trees and honeysuckle curtained the windows, making the

light in the room dim and greenish. We could see at all only because several pieces of tin had blown off the roof and light streamed in there—along with more honeysuckle.

The little cabin, Doc told us, had been built back in 1844 by a man named Adams who had come in to the settlement by covered wagon, felled and notched the trees for the log walls, roofed them with hand-rived boards, raised the rock chimney and stayed on to rear a family of a dozen children there.

Later it was to serve as the community's schoolhouse, identified in the old records as Sweet Apple school, from an apple tree which stood in the yard. Since the 1930s it had been standing vacant, inhabited only by dirt dobbers and hornets and probably an occasional field mouse or snake. A city couple had bought it along with acres of surrounding land.

"Are they going to fix it up?" I asked anxiously.

Doc said he thought they would—someday. After all, a log cabin so close to a pulsing metropolitan area like Atlanta, city of a million, must be very rare.

I may never have seen the little cabin again except for the fact that our friend Jack bought the twenty acres we had started to look at and we kept coming back. Every weekend he organized work crews to labor on the road into his woods, to clear his building site and hack down blackjacks and spindling pine saplings that impeded his view of the mountains. My children, coveys of their friends and I were delighted participants. We brought lunches and picnicked along the creek bank. We brought along iron kettles of stew and an old smoky coffeepot and feasted sumptuously by bonfires on the hilltop. The first structure erected on the land was one I supervised, a wobbly picnic table on the ground where Jack planned someday to have his house.

And every time we came, at some point during the day I would slip off in one of the cars and go look at Sweet Apple schoolhouse.

Spring came and the old-fashioned Seven Sisters roses bloomed riotously among the weeds before the plum thicket. Wild daisies crowded close to the little path, which was not quite so faint now. (We had acquired a machete for Jack's road work and I brought it along to discourage snakes.) One May day my daughter Susan and I discovered wild strawberries were ripe at Sweet Apple and the whole work party knocked off at Jack's and hurried over to pick. Within an hour or so we had filled our picnic baskets and gone back to town to dine on strawberry shortcake and turn the berries we couldn't eat into strawberry jam.

By mid-summer I was pestering Doc to find out if the owners of Sweet Apple wouldn't consider selling it to me. He tried to discourage me. The little cabin, he said, was in the middle of a sizable tract of land which Mr. and Mrs. L. A. Kalmans owned. They wouldn't dream of selling even an acre of land so situated.

"Tell them," I said desperately, "I'll give them a thousand dollars for the cabin and an acre of land!"

It was a wildly profligate gesture for me to make in 1961 when land in north Fulton County was still selling for two or three hundred dollars an acre, especially since I would have to borrow the thousand dollars. Doc and the Kalmans were apparently impressed with the depth of my feeling for Sweet Apple because within a few days the word came back: They would sell.

Sweet Apple Cabin emerges
from the wilderness

As my mother, Muv, said when she heard about it, I had as much use for a sagging old log cabin as a hog has for a saddle. And the first Saturday after I acquired it I began to suspect that she had come up with a peculiarly apt simile. Hog—pig in a poke. Saddle—on my back.

The ink on the bill of sale was barely blotted when the work crews jubilantly switched their base of operations from Jack's woods to Sweet Apple. We arrived with high hearts and the station wagon loaded to the gunwales with machetes, axes, pruning shears, saws, shovels, hoes and, of course, picnic baskets. And as we stood before it in the bright late-summer sunshine, it seemed to me I had never seen a picture of more abject desolation and dilapidation.

The weeds were taller and ranker than ever, the rusty tin roof had not only blown off in spots but what was left was worn with the absurd, tipsy, over-one-eye rakishness of a drunk's hat. Even the logs, which had seemed beautiful before, in the merciless light of the morning sun showed up cracks and rotting spots. I had seen but two of the cabin's sides because of the impenetrable wall of dead plum trees tightly laced with honeysuckle that not only lived but lived vociferously—its branches as big as a man's wrist and fairly rippling with muscle.

I had an uneasy feeling that it might be better not to inspect the whole thing fully and Doc, who had run over to see us launched, didn't improve the outlook any.

"There's an old well around here somewhere," he said casually. "Be careful you don't fall in it."

The sun was high and so were the blisters on our hands when we found the well.

Jack's uncle and our friend, Mister Willie, who was visiting from New Orleans, manned a machete and was hacking a path from the road to the back door of the cabin when his blade struck metal. He hacked away a covering tangle of old rose bushes, briars and weeds to reveal more tin roofing, obviously placed to cover something. When the boys helped him lift it, there was bared in all its glory a big round hole in the ground, at the bottom of which we beheld, like a malevolent, Cyclops eye, a scum-covered pool of water.

I didn't know then what I was to learn a little later—that water in the country is a yes-and-no, sometimes kind of thing and that such holes in the ground come high, often costing as much as I had paid for the cabin, land and all.

The discovery of the well cheered me nonetheless and to celebrate I called a break for lunch, pulled out blankets, beach towels and deck chairs and set up on the very brink of this unpromising body of water.

Later we were to picnic over every foot of the ground, cooking hotdogs over a grill made out of an old refrigerator shelf by the back door, barbecuing pork chops in the little grove of cherry trees, grilling steaks under the old apple tree which had sheltered a collapsed pole corncrib out back, dispensing sandwiches and salad from boards laid across sawhorses in any clearing we could find.

When the first fall days came we knocked off work and picked muscadines down in the hollow. This wild, sweet grape, cousin of the tawny scuppernong which grows on arbors in most southern gardens, hung in purple swags and festoons from low-growing bushes and tall pine trees. We picked as long as we could see and then went home to make grape jam, wonderful tart conserve and a few bottles of sweet dark wine.

Gradually Sweet Apple cabin began to emerge from the wilderness, standing high on its stacked rock foundations and looking a little naked and exposed without its swaddling of green. We worked joyfully, for the pure pleasure of being outdoors and bringing a kind of order to the funny little cabin and its yard. I had no plan beyond that for Sweet Apple.

My children brought their friends and I found I began to value them for what they could do. A skinny Georgia Tech student who had been hanging around my house off and on for years, listening to records with my children or working on old cars in the driveway, had never impressed me unduly before. But in the country I learned that he was willing and handy with axe and shovel, that he was intrepid about snakes and lizards, that he took an interest in June bugs and butterflies. And when he spearheaded a movement to pour a concrete apron around the well, I recognized in young Edward Bazemore a man of sterling worth.

We worked all one weekend on the concrete apron around the well and the next week Jack discovered a sale of cobblestones on an old downtown Atlanta street that was being torn up to make way for an expressway. For ten cents apiece we could have all the cobblestones we could haul. Thereafter all comers brought a few cobblestones in the trunks of their cars.

Jack, who had gone to journalism school, got a book on rock masonry at the library and reported that this old country craft could be learned as well as newswriting. He began laying a cobblestone coping for the well. I found that mixing concrete is only slightly more difficult than mixing biscuits and I could slather the damp gray filling between the cobblestones almost as easily as putting icing between the layers of a cake.

There was a special kind of satisfaction in it, too, because as I saw the well coping of rough-cut, silvered stone take shape I had a feeling of kinship with the past. The feet of Confederate soldiers had marched over those cobblestones. General Sherman and his men had no doubt littered them with ashes and charred timbers as they set fire to Atlanta. The carriage wheels of the famed editor-orator Henry Grady had rolled over them. And now they surrounded and kept safe my well.

Of course it wasn't a real, functioning well at that point. We still brought our water in jugs from town. But once the coping was up and the concrete had set, the boys decided to investigate what lay below. It was a project that held no attraction for me. As a newspaper reporter I had covered too many stories of people trapped in cave-ins and I was absolutely certain that old wells harbored snakes.

Nonsense, said Jack, donning sneakers and bathing trunks, preparatory to mounting the ladder he had set in the well. This well had hard-packed clay walls. In fact, he found the steps some earlier well digger had cut into the sides of the wall were as clearly defined and useful as they had ever been. He took a bucket and a shovel below with him and my worst fears were confirmed when the first bucketful of slime Jimmy hauled to the surface contained a snake.

It was a very little snake, Jack pointed out, and the only one down there but as soon as I could turn my chore of dumping buckets over to somebody else I quit the scene.

The well-cleaning was a highly organized operation with Jack, the underground man, setting the rules. Nobody, he decreed, would ever go in the well unless there were two people on the surface, one to lend assistance and one to go for more help if there was serious trouble. One person manned the pulley, lifting the sludge and dirty water to the surface, as Jack filled the buckets below, and a third dumped the buckets far enough down the slope so it wouldn't run back into the well. My son Jimmy's best friend, Robert, shanghaied one weekend when he wanted to laze around home, rigged up a pulley dumping system so he could sit in the station wagon and drive back and forth and the buckets would empty themselves. First it was greenish, evil-smelling water but gradually the water cleared and Jack began to dig, sending up buckets of white chalk-like kaolin as he opened up new streams and let in the sweet fresh water.

By now the chilly fall days were upon us and I swept out the cabin, tacked plastic over the open windows and tried to make it snug enough to serve as a shelter from the wind and rain. A few boards from the rubble of the old kitchen would make a fire in the fireplace that warmed half the room and drew the workers like a magnet at the end of a day in the open air. A chunk of oak or hickory, burned low, would cook a pot of soup or beef stew that was a sumptuous feast for tired people.

We brought a little gateleg table, retrieved from an apartment house garbage pile and scrubbed with lye water, and set it up before the fireplace. Deck chairs, acquired from Decatur Street secondhand stores for fifty cents each, provided seating. Sometimes, when friends came out from town to join us after we had put in a weekend of labor, we spread a red-checkered cloth over the table and set candles in wine bottles and feasted on a slab of beef roasted over the coals with a side pot of turnip greens and little corncakes cooked in the ashes.

The first Christmas I owned Sweet Apple I thought I was too busy in town to visit the little cabin but snow fell a week before Christmas—one of those snows, rare for Georgia, that covered the ground and blanketed the earth with white for days. My children and our friends insisted that we run out and look at the cabin in the snow on Christmas Eve. The reason for their insistence stood there in the yard—their Christmas gift to me. They had gone down into Doc and Verda's woods and laboriously dug up fifteen dogwood trees and transplanted them in a zigzag line between the cabin and the road!

It was the handsomest gift I ever received and I clambered out and stood with the snow sifting into my shoes and wept to see the little trees, each one with a brave tattered ensign of white flying.

Verda, the boys explained, said the secret of transplanting dogwoods was to orient them properly. She had tied a white rag on the northernmost branch of each tree before they dug it up and then followed them to the cabin to make sure they planted each tree with the flag flying on the north side.

Whether Verda's advice was sound horticulturally or some of the green thumb witchcraft I suspect she practices, it apparently worked. Now, three years later, all but three of the dogwoods live and flourish. A truck ran over two of those and somebody unloaded lumber on the third.

Tree planting is always a gesture toward the future and in more ways than one that Christmas was a turning point in my and Sweet Apple's future together. It was then that Susan told me that she wanted to marry Edward, that lanky Tech student who had been so handy with a shovel. (I don't think this had anything to do with their decision to marry in the spring when he would be getting home from the Army's engineering school at Fort Belvoir.) And when spring came we learned that Mary, my youngest daughter, had already married Cricket Fleming, another of the tribe of strong-backed youngsters who had been helping us in the country.

The day after Susan and Edward's wedding was an especially fine Sunday in May. My mother, Muv, and our friends, Julia and Sech, who had come up from the Gulf Coast to see Susan married, were still in town. In the pressure of handling the unaccustomed role of mother of the bride, I hadn't looked beyond the wedding day itself to plan anything for our guests' entertainment.

After church we had but to glance at the cornflower blue sky to know the answer: a picnic at Sweet Apple.

The ham and turkey cooked for the wedding festivities had long since vanished but I found a couple of packages of hotdogs in the refrigerator and Jack came up with two bottles of champagne left over from one of the pre-nuptial parties.

We spread lunch on the shady side of the cabin by the old chimney. Muv and Julia and Sech, discovering they were reared on some of the same old songs, cooked hotdogs, sipped champagne and sang lustily:

> I'll tune up my fiddle, I'll rosin my bow,
> I'll play sweet music wherever I go!

Our neighbor Clarence Johnson walked up the road to talk to me about plowing a spot for my garden patch. I had already been thinking how empty and lonesome the house in town was going to be with two children married and gone. And on that May day with the singing at my back and the promise of a garden before me, I began to think about a new way of life for myself.

Why not sell the house in town and move to Sweet Apple?

*The rebuilding and restoration
of Sweet Apple*

It was a frosty day in November when the rebuilding of Sweet Apple cabin actually got underway.

The sale of the old house on Thirteenth Street had been a wrenching accomplishment of the summer and I took an apartment as a sort of interim stopover to await the birth of Mary's first baby and to finish a book while we looked for builders.

Judson Carter and his first assistant, Tom Vance, of Carrollton, Georgia, were due November 5, and we all went out to meet them. Stopping only long enough for a cup of instant coffee and to wipe the frost off the windshield, we bundled into slacks and fleece-lined sweat shirts and headed out from town.

The sun was high and so benign the frost on the tin roof was beginning to melt and drip on the grass when we heard a car turn off the highway. They came like men equipped for a safari, the carpenters did. Blankets and quilts and grub boxes filled the corners of the car that weren't already filled with tools and house jacks. Messrs. Carter and Vance were on the job and prepared to stay a spell.

There were mightier building projects in the world, I knew, but the sight of these gentlemen walking around my old log house with their denim nail aprons on and rules and hammers swinging from loops on the legs of their overalls was so splendid, so portentous of achievement, I was beside myself with excitement.

Of course it's proper that building, as any new undertaking, should be exhilarating and suspenseful. There's a whole new community of interest opening before you—new friends who are attracted by the sight of walls coming up or going down, the sound of hammer and saw. There's a fresh rich vocabulary to learn. Ratsills and rafters and muntins—things a house has you never suspected before. Froes and adz, gluts and beetles—tools you never heard of. There are exotic-sounding operations—toenail this joist, shim another.

Judson Carter was our choice for rebuilding Sweet Apple because, unlike other builders, he did not begin by saying we should tear the whole thing down and start over. (My son, Jimmy, proudly showed the old cabin to a friend of his who worked on the county survey team and knew about construction. "Be mine," said the friend, "I'd stick a match to it.")

But Judson was the son of an old-time, well-respected builder in the little west Georgia town of Carrollton and he had a nice regard for old workmanship and old materials. He pledged himself to retain every inch of the existing structure that was sound and to shore up what was left. His lieutenant, Tom Vance, was a man in his seventies who knew from experience vital things about notching logs and "kivvering" a roof, not with ersatz composition materials or even with boughten shingles but with "boards," those tapered slices of wood that are rived from the heart of a giant white oak tree.

From time to time they recruited other workmen—one fellow memorable chiefly for his name, "Horse Collar," and eventually our neighbor Quinton Johnson, who has continued to be a source of strength and help on every subsequent Sweet Apple building project.

All the neighbors became interested—both the citified, suburban types, who, like us, moved out from town and came in their station wagons to kibbitz, and the old settlers, whose ancestors came down from the mountains a couple of hundred years ago and who continue to live pretty much as their forebears lived.

Our first callers, except for Doc and Verda, were Clarence and Olivia Johnson, who live up on the paved road and came bearing gifts—a sack of sweet potatoes from their garden and a windlass for the well. Our second caller was Mrs. Fred Stiles, whose husband is an executive at the Lockheed plant twenty miles away. She arrived in a pickup truck with a bushel basket of plants and bulbs, a sack of fertilizer and a shovel to help me plant them.

Mr. Lum Crow, Olivia Johnson's father, became one of our most cherished friends and helpers. A man then approaching his eightieth birthday, he walked down the road with the erect easy tread of an Indian. He had attended school at Sweet Apple back in the 90s, known several generations of people who had moved in and out of it and hunted rabbits around it in the thirty years it was lonely and untenanted.

It was Mr. Crow who helped us find some of the boards we used to reroof the cabin. Sharp-eyed and "noticing," as he himself would say, he remembered a stack of white oak boards weighted down with rocks and seasoning in a barnyard over Alpharetta way and he led us to it. Later when I learned of more boards in an old buggy house at an abandoned farm forty-five miles away, Mr. Crow went with me to help me load them on a truck we hired from another neighbor, Clint Goodman.

Mr. Crow is a prime traveling companion. His bright unclouded blue eyes take in everything, the shape and color of the earth, a hawk circling a chicken yard, ice on the river, the way chimney smoke travels straight up, denoting the stillness of the air, the pattern cattle make in a tawny winter pasture.

His comments, like his movements, are spare but eloquent. Of an ailing woman relative he said simply: "She used to be a fine-looking woman—weighed over two hundred pounds. Now, pore as a snake."

When he saw the old shingles still standing in the neat airy stacks where a thrifty farmer, now dead, had put them forty years before, Mr. Crow's judgment was like an accolade.

"Them's good boards," he said.

Working beside him is a privilege. He has an unhurried economy of movement which is grace itself. He and I stood in the bed of the truck, stacking shingles as Clint brought them from the shed and handed them up. There was ice on the ground and in the air but the sun came out and, caught up in the rhythm of reaching, lifting, stacking, we were soon red-faced and sweating and had to shuck off our jackets.

There was a bountiful supply of the boards—"enough to roof the settlemint," said Mr. Crow—and we proudly hauled them back to the cabin, where Judson and his men were already at work on the housetop.

Nailing boards on one's own roof is not a privilege vouchsafed every woman, but it was mine. New Year's Day found all of us at Sweet Apple, the real carpenters, the volunteers and Mr. Crow and I, on the roof. There were some predictions that I would: 1. Fall off the scaffold. 2. Catch my death of cold up there in the chill north wind. 3. Beat my thumbs to a bloody pulp.

There were times when they were almost right. I didn't fall but my legs were sore for days from climbing up and down the ladder with armloads of shingles and my fingers weren't comfortable on the typewriter keys for some time. The trick, of course, is in hammering. If you bend a nail and have to wrench it out, that's hard. Pulling it out of the heart of seasoned oak recruits muscles you didn't know you possessed.

But as long as all goes well, the hammer obediently falls where you aim and the nail docilely enters the wood straight and true, the job is really no more taxing than embroidery work. In fact, it has some aspects in common with needlework. You have to select and fit your boards together with reasonable care, being sure that where two meet a third covers the crack.

Judson was particular about having things lined up straight and before he gave me my hammer and my head he stretched a line across the roof to mark the boundary of the first course of shingles. After that he made chalk lines for each successive course.

The roof on Sweet Apple cabin still has a slight resemblance to a drunk's hat—a go-funny list that no amount of measuring and finagling around with plumb lines could alter. I think it has something to do with the basic, stubborn character of the cabin itself. But I love it and at night when I hear the rain on it I remember the winter day when I helped to roof it—the sharp bite of oak through my work gloves, the fragrance of seasoned wood, its grain faintly amber and rose in the light, the companionship of my fellow toilers and, when we were finished, the tart little red apples Mr. Crow passed out to refresh us.

The dark and mysterious forces of delay

The winter of Sweet Apple cabin's restoration was a bad one for Georgia. We had electricity. The Rural Electrification people came and set up a pole in the yard and one of our neighbors, Mr. Grady Daniel, an old-time electrician, put in a drop cord in the ceiling and a couple of wall outlets where the carpenters could plug in an old refrigerator and a little hot plate Muv sent me from her pantry. We put a mail-order pump in the well and ran a hose to the back door so water was accessible to the campers.

But there would come days when the rains fell, the wind roared and the temperature tumbled, chilling the marrow of your bones and turning the water which dripped from the hose into ice. Then Judson and his crew would pack up their tools and go home to the warmth of their homes in Carrollton.

And usually before they left Judson would shoot me a look which said as plain as anything: "Chinking."

I would smile and wave them off, saying nothing, but I knew that the old argument, Authenticity versus Comfort, was on again. And that wench, Nature, had chosen up sides against me.

Judson contended that my cabin, in order to be habitable, must have chinking of mortar and clay between the logs. I said no chinking.

Judson cited his authorities. Every log house he had ever seen had the cracks chinked with mud and mortar. Mine had never been chinked. Mr. Crow was my authority. When he was a pupil at Sweet Apple school, he told me, they often had to pull the boards from over the cracks in the logs to let in enough light to study by.

I made two concessions. I agreed to caulking the cracks on the inside with a white substance that matched the once whitewashed walls. This was a chore that Jimmy undertook on weekends. One day Doc watched as Jimmy pumped the caulking compound into cracks and then he pointed out a sizable hole.

"When you get here, Jim," he said, "you'd better put in gun and all."

Doc was an indispensable aid in all our undertakings, lending us his boundless energy and good humor along with tools and building materials, and even food and drink, as our need arose.

Watching the crack caulking one day, I turned to him for reassurance.

"Doc, do you think a snake could get through that hole?" I asked anxiously.

"Yes," said Doc cheerfully. "If you tried you might be able to get one through there."

My other concession to Comfort, as against Authenticity, was a mail-order fuel oil heater. I knew there would be days when I didn't have time to build a fire in the fireplace and I was willing to give over a little space in the big room to a

tacky oil burner which, with its gold-looking grill top and
bottom, looked about as much at home in a primitive log
cabin as Oleg Cassini would at a country hog-killing. It em-
barrassed me by its presence but in the home of mountain
friends, Herbert and Frances Tabor, I had seen similar heaters
make vast, drafty rooms snug and summery. And I was
hopeful.

(It developed that my instinct was right. The heater made
the upstairs bedroom and bath that we fashioned from the
loftroom oppressively hot, while water turned to ice in the
kitchen kettle and plants froze four feet away on the living-
room table. We subsequently had to replace it with an in-
credibly citified convenience, a furnace.)

When the weather permitted, work went along at a good
clip at Sweet Apple. The day the old lopsided windows in
the main room were straightened up, framed and outfitted
with sashes of glass was a great milestone to me. I remembered stories from my childhood of a great aunt who married
a rich widower and went to live in his big house. In the first
letter she wrote home, as Muv told it, she headed the roster
of her new elegances by saying: "I'm sitting up here looking
out my glass winders."

The day the "winders" went in Sweet Apple cabin I raced
inside to look out through them. Then I had to hurry out,
barking my shins over lumber and skidding on wet clay ex-
cavations, to look *in* through them. I knew just how rich
Aunt Roseanne had felt.

You forget, when you're used to it, what a beautifully func-
tional, true thing a piece of glass is. All these months rains
and wind had made free with that crazy opening in the logs,

where there used to be a wooden shutter. Birds and grass-hoppers flew in. Honeysuckle and, I suspected, snakes had climbed in. Itinerant foxhounds, getting a whiff of our ham-burgers as they pursued old Reynard, had detoured through the windows, clearing the rotting sill with the ease of Queen Elizabeth's favorite hunter taking a hurdle.

Even visiting children found egress through the window more interesting and easier than through the door. I suppose it was habit because for years the front door had been nailed shut and the back door dragged so it took a strong man with a crowbar to swing it open.

But no more. We had windows with panes of glass that let in the sunshine and the view and kept out all else. It was a happy time for me.

And then we got to the little windows which were to go upstairs—four of them, replacing two foot-square holes in the gable ends of the house. About that time I read in a magazine about some homeowners who lived in a house designed by the fabled Frank Lloyd Wright and professed to have learned from him "the joy of discontent."

This joy is no stranger to most women, who take pleasure in rearranging things often. I inherited a fair measure of it from my mother, Muv, who has been known to get up from her sickbed and start tearing down a wall—an instant, decisive discontent.

The trouble with my discontent was that I kept deciding I didn't like something after the last nail had been driven and the carpenter had straightened up to admire his work. Those upstairs windows were an example. I didn't know what I wanted in the bedroom but I felt that since log cabins had not had glass at all I should be restrained in my use of it.

When the windows for my loftroom came they were little and I thought they would do until I saw them in. After many man-hours of measuring and hammering and sawing I took a look at them and my heart sank. They were fine, conveniently arranged, well-insulated windows—and they might have come out of a pink stucco Florida motel.

I moped around about that until everybody agreed that it was better to change them than to have them stuck in my eye like a mote for years to come. The fact that that change —and all the others that I thought of belatedly—was expensive didn't surprise anybody but me.

Everybody who has ever built anything or, worse yet, remodeled anything knows that there are dark and mysterious forces of delay working against you. The aim of these forces is to keep people who tinker with old houses from ever finishing.

I had hoped to be in Sweet Apple cabin by Christmas, within two months after we started remodeling. Christmas came and I was still in the apartment in town but we visited Sweet Apple once during the holidays, clearing sawdust and lumber from around the fireplace and picnicking grandly on roast duck and white wine.

Every new development reinforced my optimism. The roof, the windows, the leveling and replacing of rotten logs with sound ones—a gift from Garland and Gloria Byrd from an old house they tore down in middle Georgia—were affirmative signs. Jack found a wrecking yard that had some ancient beams which could be sawed into flooring and I thought the end was in sight when the wide pine boards went down over the rough floor with its uphill-downhill contours, cracks and holes that had been patched with Prince Albert tobacco cans.

They framed in a new shedroom for a kitchen, to replace the one that had rotted away years before. The electrician came back and ran wires all around. The ladder that led to the loftroom was replaced with a real stairway and Judson found a niche above it for a bathroom and one beneath it for a half bath.

The plumber came. Outside under the apple trees, where the plumbing fixtures we had bought secondhand out of a wrecked Atlanta mansion waited to be installed, it got wet and cold and he found the toilets had filled with water, frozen and cracked.

For every accomplishment there seemed to be a setback. The magnificent chimney which had warmed us through our labors went out of service one of the coldest days in the year. We had raised the roof a few inches to give more headroom upstairs and that shook up the equilibrium of that little section of bricks which topped the rock chimney. The whole upper section had to be torn down and reset.

We used old brick but when Quinton Johnson had set them in place with mortar instead of clay, the effect was distractingly new. Our friend Henri Jova, an Atlanta architect who sometimes looked in on our progress on weekends, advised a bath of buttermilk and cow manure for the new section to age it and start a mellowing patina of moss. (This was a recipe we later tried with success on the bricks of the terrace.)

It was April by the time we got to painting. Some of the boards which covered the cracks in the logs had to be new—so many had fallen off with the passage of the years—and the problem of matching these to the weathered logs engrossed us. For the interior of the kitchen we were lucky to be allowed to rip hand-planed boards from the walls of antebellum Alpharetta hotel, which was being torn down. These, put up with the rough side out, were just right—warmly red seasoned pine. But the exterior of the kitchen was finished with rough new boards and battens and these, too, seemed to thwart every effort we made to match them to the old logs.

Gray stain looked like an obvious answer but there were many shades of gray—French, which was bluish; charcoal, which was too black; driftwood, which was too white; and battleship, which was altogether wrong. Our decorator friend, Edmund Bocock, looked at our efforts and said lightly, "Rub a little dirt into it." So we tried lampblack and agreed that it was closer and in time, maybe a hundred years, the new would match the old.

It was patently silly, I realized when I looked at those old logs, for us to think we'd find their color on a paint store chart. They have the silver of frost on them, the white of sun-bleached bones, the black of rainy nights on their rough-hewn old flanks. There's a bit of ochre where the wood has cracked and the pine heart shows through—and a frosting of green where lichens have taken hold. A drift of plum blossoms dusted some of the cracks with pollen gold and a butterfly wing stained another with amber. When you look at them closely the old logs are not gray at all but the color of time and the weather.

It was the middle of May when we moved in at Sweet Apple. It seemed to me later that we should have done it with ceremony like a tree-planting by the mayor or a ribbon-cutting by the governor but the whole thing was as simple and casual as beans and bread. The truck brought our furniture from the apartment and high on the stack of things we unloaded was an RFD type mailbox from the hardware store.

Jimmy used a little brush and some of the flat black paint left over from something else to letter our name on it. And then he found a post and borrowed Doc's posthole digger and when I came home from work there it was—our mailbox, brand new and clean, tidy red tin flag to the side, waiting by the highway in a cluster of others for the coming of the mail-man.

Thus our residence in the country became formal and official, blessed by the telephone company, the Cobb County Electric and the United States government.

It brought a lump to my throat when we drove up in the twilight and saw it standing there—our first country mailbox, our stake in a new place, symbol of our at-homeness.

The Sweet Apple "Settlemint"

Atlanta people are prone to confuse Sweet Apple with the little community to the east of us called Crabapple. Crab-apple is a full-fledged village with a post office, stores, churches, a community house where we who live in Sweet Apple go to vote, and a school to which our neighbors' children are hauled by bus.

Sweet Apple, on the other hand, is not really a settlement but a state of mind. I would have thought the name applied only to my cabin except that now and then you hear some old-timer use the name largely and expansively as if it applied to a vast and heavily populated area.

There was the lady whose husband went hunting with some of the neighbors and, it being a cold and raw night, was persuaded to fight off pneumonia by nipping along at a local product known as "white whiskey."

So outraged was the lady by what she took to be the evil influence of low companions that she dashed off a note to the revenuers in Atlanta saying: "Come at once. *Sweet Apple is floating in whiskey!*"

The feds did not respond as speedily as she had expected

so she followed through with what was a desperate measure in that day when phones were few and a call to Atlanta was long distance. She telephoned the revenuers.

In a day or two one of our neighbors found her bureau drawers being turned out by some gentlemen with a search warrant. The fact that they found a jug of recent vintage white whiskey and made a case against her was distressing but she didn't hold it against their informant. It was, she confided to me lately, only what you might expect of somebody who never knew the joy of warming spirits on a cold night.

Old-timers are really the only ones you hear speak of Sweet Apple as a section. They are the ones who either went to school in my log house or in the "new" Sweet Apple school, a little one-roomer which parents in the community built about the turn of the century up at the crossroads and which served until its consolidation with Ebenezer and Crabapple schools in the 1920s.

As far as I can learn there never was a store or a post office at Sweet Apple and the nearest churches are Ebenezer Methodist and Union Primitive Baptist a couple of miles away. Our mail is delivered by rural carrier out of the town of Woodstock ten miles away in another county. Before the advent of RFD the closest post office was in the house of the late Enoch Chamlee down the road, where our friends Erle Miles, an Eastern Airlines pilot, and his wife, Maude, now live. Named for Mr. Chamlee and his father, also called Enoch, the post office was Big Enoc, Georgia. (The government unaccountably dropped the final "H". Mr. Chamlee's daughter, Jettie Bell Johnson, can but speculate that the name was too long for the signboard they happened to have at the time.)

The "settlemint," as Mr. Crow calls it, is to me all the neighbors that I see frequently and all that area that I can get to easily, lying roughly between the Canton highway and the curve of Little River. Cox Road, paved in the 1950s, is our main thoroughfare. It runs from the Canton highway, where little Ebenezer Methodist Church and its old grave-yard stand, a distance of about two miles to the Cherokee County line where the pavement ends right at the old Chamlee place, which the Mileses bought and remodeled in the 1940s. Their house, originally a log cabin, too, is on the edge of a beautiful expanse of woods and pastureland stretching down to Little River in the back and facing the blue silhouette of Brushy Mountain (sometimes called Sweat Mountain) in front.

Along Cox Road are the homes of numbers of people named Cox, Dangar and Johnson, all old families. From it we turn off to go to Mr. and Mrs. Crow's, to Doc and Verda's, to the Sam Brazeals' and the Fred Stiles', to Jack's and his neighbors, the Holders', and to Sweet Apple.

In recent years a sprinkling of brick ranch houses has gone up along Cox Road, some built by newcomers from the city and some by the sons and daughters of old settlers who have bought or been given land from old homesteads.

At the other end of the river's curve, where the Canton highway crosses it, is our source of supplies, our wellspring of information and news, our social center—Chadwick's store. If you need to know where to get martin gourds in the spring you drop by Chadwick's. ("Philip Hughes, across the river and just beyond Big Springs Church, had some last week.")

If you want a special size basket made out of white oak splits or some porch rockers recaned you ask at Chadwick's. ("Mr. Jim Taylor on Arnold Mill Road, just before you get to that big chicken house outside Woodstock, is your man.") If there's a land auction, a church supper or a horse sale, notice is posted in Chadwick's window.

Chadwick's store, in one building or another, has been there by the river since before the Cherokee Indians were banished from north Georgia. Aubrey Chadwick, his wife, Ruby, and their son, Gerald, run it now. Aubrey's father, William Washington Chadwick—called Wash—ran it before him and before that Aubrey's great-grandfather, Billy Chamlee, ran it.

Wagon trains coming down from the mountains camped near the store or its neighbor, Arnold's grist mill. Drovers herding cattle, hogs or turkeys ahead of them to sell in Atlanta stopped and traded with Grandpa Chamlee.

The old man was what we call hereabouts "a turrible churchman," which is to say devout.

In his day part of Saturday and all of Sunday were set aside as days of worship and only a stranger from a great distance would expect to do any trading with Grandpa Chamlee on Saturday morning. They tell of a mountain man who made the mistake of driving up with a load of corn to swap for rations one Saturday morning and caught Grandpa hitching up to go to meeting.

"You and your corn just set tight," said Mr. Chamlee. "I'll tend to you after meeting."

He took off for Providence Baptist Church five or six miles away and didn't return until after several hours of preaching and praying.

The same casual, leisurely treatment of customers still prevails at Chadwick's, which makes tense, hurried suburban types fidget and chafe when they first encounter it. But Dr. and Mrs. Bernard Wolff, who have a weekend place on a lake down my road, declare that picking out a steak at Chadwick's or being fitted for work shoes or a new garden tractor is always the beginning of relaxation for them. There's no such thing as a hurried transaction.

In the midst of buying flower seed I am prepared to wander across the road with Ruby and pick a mess of turnips out of her garden or collect a few flower cuttings. I have walked off and left a half-filled grocery cart to trail Aubrey down through a barnyard and over a pasture fence back of the store to visit the old abandoned graveyard where the only legible "tomb rock" standing marks the grave of the man whose son built my cabin. This was James Adams, a private in the Third South Carolina regiment, during the Revolutionary War. His son, Mastin Adams, built my cabin. Another son, Matthew, married Evaline Hughes Reese, a young widow, whose daughter, granddaughter and great-grandsons, the big Dangar clan, still live along Cox Road on land acquired in 1830.

One of the Saturday attractions at Chadwick's is Mr. Tom Fincher's impromptu barbering service on the front porch. In the midst of nail kegs and fence wire and sacks of feed and fertilizer Mr. Fincher cuts the hair of the men in the settlement and enlivens the time between customers by playing on his jew's-harp.

The jokes about city folks who have worn stocking caps an entire summer to hide one of his haircuts never bother Mr. Fincher, who is known as one of the kindest, jolliest men in the community. They say that no neighbor is ever ill but what

Tom Fincher shows up to milk his cows, feed his stock and haul in firewood for him. Once when I had car trouble on my way to Chadwick's, Mr. Fincher took his truck and towed my disabled vehicle home and would not accept pay.

"You just come spend a spell with Ida Belle and me," he said hospitably. "We'll treat you so many different ways one of 'em is bound to suit you."

Between Chadwick's at the north end of the curve and the Mileses' at the south end, Little River meanders through a heavily wooded section that has some pretty hills from which you can, on a clear day, see the Blue Ridge Mountains. One such lookout is called "Johnson's rock"—a great gray slab of granite jutting out from a hill over the river itself. Mr. Crow walked a bunch of us to Johnson's rock one Sunday in the early spring before the leaves were out but when the hillside was white with dogwood blooms. From the rock we could easily see farmhouses and fields miles across the river in what is known as "Rusk country," the community where Secretary of State Dean Rusk was born and where his brother, the Miami newspaperman Parks Rusk, still maintains a home.

Old house sites abound in the woods around Sweet Apple. One on the Mileses' land, but nearer to Jack's house than theirs, was once the home of a Rusk cousin, remembered now only by his nickname, Purg Rusk. We always walk over there at least once in the spring because, although the house has long since been torn down, the dooryard is outlined by borders of old-fashioned daffodils and the fragrant little "butter and eggs" that bloom faithfully every March. And near the pile of rocks where there was once an old chimney a crabapple tree perfumes the air deliciously.

The rough wagon road to Johnson's rock is now used

mainly by fox hunters—not the stylish horsemen who ride to the hounds and hold their meets on Chattahoochee plantations every year but rough-clad men who bring their dogs out in pickup trucks, release them and sit by a campfire and listen to them run. The hillside by the rock is littered with the remnants of long-dead fires where legions of hunters have warmed the outer man while passing a bottle or cups of strong coffee to warm the inner man and listened to the music of dogs called Blue and Babe running on some distant hill.

When Jettie Bell Johnson (nee Chamlee) was a little girl back about World War I, the land which now runs mostly to woods and pasture was heavily cultivated. Hundreds of acres of it had belonged to the Merritt family until shortly after the Civil War and was subsequently divided among married children, including some of the Coxes, or sold. Every sizable farm had one or more tenant houses. In this near-mountainous area the tenants or "renters" were always white, never Negro, although Roswell, only six miles away, was settled by slave-owning aristocrats from the coast and there is now a fair-sized Negro population made up of the descendants of these slaves.

Even as recently as her childhood, Jettie Bell recalls that Sweet Apple section was cut off from the outside world by the condition of the roads. Her father went to Roswell once or twice a year to get supplies but all of the food, except sugar and coffee, was raised on the place.

Atlanta was an unthinkable distance away—so far that Jettie Bell was a teen-ager living in Roswell to attend high school before it ever occurred to her to make the trip. Even today for every half dozen people who commute to jobs in Atlanta there are two or three who haven't been to the city in ten or twenty years. There are probably a few like the late Miss Lovie Keener, who lived a little farther up in the mountains and never got to Atlanta at all. She heard about it and thought of it some but when I offered to take her to see the city she shook her head.

"No, much obliged," she said. "Hit's too fur to walk and cars jiggle you so bad."

Old settlers around Sweet Apple know the art of self-sufficiency. They were reared to grow or make what they needed and the old skills of killing and curing their own meats, drying and preserving fruits and vegetables, are still practiced to a degree. Joel Smith, who also lives just off Cox Road and works on the county roads regularly, is greatly in demand in the wintertime for his skill as a butcher. When the wind is still and the temperature drops in December and January, somebody in the community calls on Joel to preside over a hog-killing.

This is a time of festivity today as it was in the old days, when all the neighbors gathered to lend a hand and to feast before the day was over on home-canned vegetables, dried apple pies, fresh pork and, if the "rendering" went well, hot corn bread made rich and crunchy with fresh cracklings—the bits of pork from which lard is made.

Corn-shuckings, barn-raisings, log-rollings and quilting bees were still a part of life in this community long after they had been forgotten in most places so close to an urban area. Candy-pullings were events of Jettie Bell's childhood and she remembers that when it was too cold or the roads were too bad for the young people to gather to cook the syrup and pull the candy her mother would often make a pan of peanut brittle from home-grown peanuts and home-grown sorghum.

Jettie Bell's uncle, Mr. Wheeler Westbrook, who was born in 1889 and attended school in my log cabin for at least a year, remembers that every year somebody in the settlement had new ground to clear. Brush was always piled up at the edge of the fields and in the fall when birds sought refuge in it the sport of "bird knocking" was greatly enjoyed by the men and boys of the community.

Lighted pine knots were thrown into the brush and as the birds took to their wings the skillful pitchers in the crowd knocked them down with more knots or rocks.

"When the brush fire burned low we had the birds cleaned and roasted them over the coals on long sticks," recalls Mr. Westbrook. "It didn't matter what kind of bird it was, we ate them all."

The Indians had been gone from the country only about fifty years when Mr. Westbrook was a boy and the fields were still littered with arrowheads and fragments of their pottery. Today but two Indian mounds are left—one in the Mileses' pasture and one in the woods beyond the old Westbrook place, now occupied by the Sam Brazeals. After a rain a child looking for a rock for his slingshot may still pick up an arrowhead instead.

Sweet Apple as a "settlemint" may be a place shaped by memory and fleshed out by nostalgia but some of us believe in it. That's why partly to make it real, partly in fun we all defer to Jettie Bell's lively and entertaining "Unc," Mr. Westbrook, as "the mayor of Sweet Apple," bow to him deferentially when we meet on the road and say, "Good day to you, Mister Mayor."

It's very likely that Doc started this custom because he insists, with a leer, that he's the second man in the hierarchy of Sweet Apple government.

"I'm the *vice* mayor," says Doc.

Life in the country

The first month I was in Sweet Apple cabin a reader wrote in to ask with some amusement, "Do you really claim in this convenience and comfort-laden twentieth century that there is any difference in life thirty miles from a big city?"

Right away I thought of one difference. About the second night I crawled into bed in the slanted roofed little bedroom at Sweet Apple and turned on my light to read a bit. I had that feeling everybody has experienced of being stared at. I glanced at the window and sure enough, there was a little beige and brown snake peering through the screen with unmistakable interest.

He was gone by the time I yelled up Jimmy from downstairs and he had trained a flashlight on the rock chimney outside the window.

I had my sleepless nights in the city, of course, but I never recall lying awake worrying about snakes looking in the window.

There are special, different country interruptions, too. Like the afternoon I was raking the yard and one of the boys remarked conversationally: "That's a pretty yellow-bellied flycatcher but he's going to mess up the plumbing."

"What?" I asked out of routine politeness—the way you do when somebody had just said a perfectly senseless thing.

He pointed and what he had said made abundant sense. A little bird was assiduously and methodically hauling straw and sticks and putting it in the bathroom vent pipe which stuck out through the roof. I dropped my rake and headed for the ladder and the top of the roof with a wire basket—one I meant to plant flowers in but which now screens the vent pipe from nesting birds.

It wasn't the kind of thing that ever happened to me on Thirteenth Street.

It's true that life in the country, at least as we live it, has certain comforts and conveniences nowadays. The appliance repairman from Rich's big store in Atlanta nearly fell out of his truck one day when I flagged him down in the road and told him the dishwasher he was looking for was in my house.

"In *there?*" he cried, pointing unbelievingly at my log cabin.

I have a washing machine and a dryer, too, although I didn't acquire them at once. While we were still working on the well we received a visit from Mrs. Ruth Stevens, who with her late husband had lived at Sweet Apple back in the 1930s. She told me it was "a good well of water" and that she always had the prettiest, whitest washes when she lived at Sweet Apple.

"I had my pot right there," she said, pointing to a spot near the well. "You need you a black iron pot, too."

Tom Vance later brought me an iron pot and I usually keep geraniums in it in the summertime. I tried hauling the laundry to washaterias in town for a while and it wasn't hard work, as little Mrs. Stevens knew it, just uninteresting and onerous. I'd a sight rather have done my washing standing barefoot in a creek and beating the sheets on a rock than have to fight for a parking space and then stand in line at a counter to get unknown, unseen hands to stuff my clothes in a machine.

But then I got a machine of my own and I discovered it was a mighty companionable thing. At night before I go to bed I frequently put a load of clothes in it and the sound of it chugging away out there in the little utility house is very cheerful and friendly. At first I was like my mountain friend, Aunt Nancy Pankey, when she stopped cooking on the hearth and traded a little heifer for her first "four-eyed arn cookstove." It couldn't function properly because she kept taking the lids off to be sure the fire was burning. I kept lifting the lid of my washer just to see what was going on in there.

Now I don't interfere with its work but once I have relieved it of the clean clothes, if it's a sunny day I hang them on the line and keep finding excuses to linger in the back yard and admire them. Even ironing isn't as bad as it used to be in the city because the clothes come in from a country line smelling of clover and wild strawberries and new-cut grass.

Differences?

It takes a year of living any place to know its faces and moods, to partake of its full flavor. So here is a year's sampling of life at Sweet Apple, put down as it happened:

Winter

It takes all kinds of equipment to begin a journey into a new year. I leave to preachers and other wise men the task of telling us pilgrims what to put in our mental and emotional knapsacks for the trip. But there's one strictly material possession I can strongly recommend for the coming year: a thermometer.

I went to the dime store and bought a splendid big one with a magnified face that I can read through the window.

Mark Twain spoke of the "sumptuous variety" of New England weather, which "compels the stranger's admiration and regret." New England weather may hold the record for extremes but there's a lot of room between extremes for variety and Sweet Apple weather gallops back and forth between heavenly and horrible.

Think of keeping a finger on the pulse of all the weather that the new year holds for us—and to speak plummeting or soaring temperatures with authority gained from one's very own thermometer.

A big wind came some time in the night and whistled down the chimney, blowing ashes out on the hearth, rattling panes and causing the two pine trees which grow up through the kitchen eaves to creak and moan like the rigging on a four-masted schooner in full gale. We stirred and listened once or twice, were grateful for the warmth and snugness of the cabin and turned over and went back to sleep.

The next morning I went out to find two casualties—the big old dead chinaberry tree and the new clothesline.

The loss of the old dead tree really hurt me. I loved that old hulk reared up against the sky, its trunk and branches silvered and shaggy with lichens, pockmarked by the tireless riveting of woodpeckers. And nothing apparently delights a mockingbird more than a high clear perch for his serenades. The mockingbirds had regarded that old chinaberry as their personal soapbox.

More than that, there was the wisteria vine I was training to climb on that tree. Now I'll have to find another standard for it.

As for the clothesline, I couldn't be gladder to see anything go. It was one of those fancy folding things of aluminum with arms like a television antenna that I bought under the silly notion that it was desirable to hide the laundry. Right away I hated it. In the country where there's plenty of space and nobody to note nor long remember the condition of my underwear and household linen, it's silly to be squinchy with sunshine and air.

Now it's gone. Bent and twisted and broken by the fall of the chinaberry tree. I fished it out and hauled it to the dump and Jack arrived with a power saw to cut up the tree into fireplace lengths. I'll miss the tree, all right, but it's not a complete loss. Chinaberry wood, like Edna St. Vincent Millay's candles, gives a lovely light.

Compared to moon shots and marches and some of the other urgent, history-making things that are going on elsewhere in the world, life at Sweet Apple would seem intolerably placid and uneventful to some people. But we do have our excitements. Wood-getting is one of these.

Now wood for a fireplace is different from just fuel to warm your house. It's nice and usually efficient to have oil for the furnace and I don't knock it, particularly on a bitter morning when I step out of bed onto a warm floor.

But wood for the fireplace warms the spirit and pleasures all the senses, particularly the eyes and the nose. A good fire is a whole picture gallery to look at and the fragrance of the different kinds of wood is as subtle and soothing as incense from the Orient.

An important part of the satisfaction of a good fire is getting the wood oneself, being outdoors on a bright cold day, listening to the song of the power saw, smelling the sharp pungent fragrance of sawdust and hefting and hauling the logs.

There's an old house site over in the woods and near the rubble of its fallen chimney and rock foundations a long-dead cedar tree. Jack came by in the truck with his power saw and asked if we wanted to go get the old tree for the fireplace. We couldn't get into blue jeans and sweaters and scarves fast enough.

It was a lovely old tree with its driftwood-colored branches and when the saw bit into its twisted trunk it had a deep rose heart and a heavenly cedar smell . . . of pencils you used to take to school, of the water bucket in the mountains, of your mama's blankets and quilts the first cool night in October.

I picked out branches to save because they were pretty and

starred with moss like little green medallions. I'm hoarding the logs, too, rationing myself to burn only one piece of cedar an evening and then for very special company.

My annual cold, the big one, hit me and I had some vague idea of beating it by crawling in bed and waiting it out. For some reason this seems to enrage a cold and bring out all its more virulent aspects and by the second day I was coughing with the resonance and frequency of an old, old bullfrog croaking on a summer night. And my chest hurt.

Susan came out to nurse me and I found myself wishing for fried cloths on my chest like Muv used to apply. Susan laughed at smelly wool rags in this day of miracle drugs and left the room to get me another archaic nostrum, hot lemonade. I fell into a broody silence.

Fried cloths probably weren't efficacious but when you had one of them on your chest you sure felt something was being done for you. I forget how Muv made them but I believe suet and turpentine, or possibly kerosene, were all mixed up in an old iron skillet, and wool rags big enough to cover the chest were sort of sautéed in the mixture. You had one on your chest, one freshly heated on the way to you and one simmering in the skillet, and the whole thing was uncomfortable and aromatic enough to assure the sufferer that drastic steps were being taken in his behalf.

Even while I lay a-bed dreaming of fried cloths, Mrs. Lois P. Newman of Tallapoosa, Georgia, was dispatching a note to me about light'ard knots in which she pointed out their use for treatment of colds and pneumonia, as well as for fire starting.

Her recipe: "You take an old cast-iron teakettle and place

it over a small pit or on rocks so that the spout is tipped forward. Put rich light'ard splinters inside and build a hot fire underneath, being careful not to let the splinters catch fire. Soon the brown pungent liquid will flow from the 'kittle' spout. It will keep indefinitely when stored in a bottle or can and only has to be warmed and it is ready to soak flannel for chest poultices."

The death of Sophie Tucker brought a special twinge of regret to me—not because I knew Miss Tucker personally or anything like that. I didn't. But I always admired her from afar and when I acquired my "arn cookstove" for Sweet Apple, looking at its rather substantial lines, I hopefully named it Sophie. My stove, an old-timer like the real Sophie, would, I thought, merit the designation "Last of the Red-Hot Mamas."

Well, maybe Sophie Tucker, the woman, lived up to that name. But Sophie, my stove, has not.

She is small, as such stoves went, but she has the regulation four "eyes" of the big stove, an oven big enough to accommodate a pan of biscuits or a ham, and the regulation warming oven up top. All she really lacks is the hot-water reservoir.

But she has two faults. She does not get hot—at least not hot enough to warm my rather big and draughty kitchen, which is the reason I acquired her in the first place. And she has an unfortunate habit of smoking and spitting soot.

Various people have suggested remedies for this—the most frequent being to raise the pipe, the nastiest to get rid of Sophie altogether. Well, we tried raising the pipe but it didn't work and I refuse to get rid of Sophie because in spite of her failings I've become attached to her. She's so cute looking. She may not bake the rolls but she will warm the dinner plates and she does make the kettle to sing and invite me to pull up a rocker beside her and toast my toes, even while sifting soot down my collar.

Since my mother, Muv, discovered the telephone I get very few of those fat, clipping-filled letters written in the slanty backhand script which I used to cherish. In a way I'm sorry, because Muv was a great letter writer, one who put flavor as well as the substance of the news in her letters. I always enjoyed her enclosures, too. Sometimes it would be a sprig of something blooming in her yard, sometimes the recipe for the cake which made such a hit at the Woman's Society for Christian Service, and sometimes a bit of doggerel which she would compose on the spot to illustrate some point she made.

For years Muv considered long-distance telephone an extravagance warranted only in the case of death, illness or a sudden influx of company.

Now, of course, tolls aren't so prohibitive and Muv has accepted the telephone and uses it comfortably and often—until she gets a bill that appalls her. Then for thirty days and nights she avoids the telephone as if it were a typhoid carrier.

Even when I call her she backs away from the phone to talk and in the midst of my best nuggets of news she will say, "Well, this is costing money . . . goodbye!" and flings the receiver on the hook from what I judge to be a great distance.

Sometimes I think letter writing is really the most satisfactory way to communicate with Muv.

The stark, line drawing quality of the landscape is at its best in February. Here there is little concealment, little blurring of details. I like to walk in February and if you set out in the late afternoon you can be practically certain that if there's a good sunset you won't miss it. Only the dark green of the pines and the soft brown shoulder of a hill obscure the sun's final moments—and then to give it the proper frame and focus.

My own scant and scraggly acres, which now number almost five, interest me particularly these days. It's pleasant to walk down past the old sawdust pile and admire the corky gray branches of a small forest of sweetgum trees. Now, better than at any other time, you can see the shape of the dogwoods and assess by the number of pearl gray buttons on the branches what the crop of blossoms will be along about April.

Patches of broom sedge are not welcome when they pop up in the garden or on the lawn in summer, but now they are a lovely amber color, softening the severe black and gray of tree trunk and bare branch.

There's a hill I admire because of the pine knots I found there one winter and the big golden-eyed violets that grow there in the spring. Now it shows me rocks, beautiful lichened rocks that shelter a few ferns, and clear, clean-washed bits of rock that hold within themselves the jewel tones of precious stones. I keep meaning to find out about rocks, to know their names and what they are good for, but so far I've never gotten beyond filling my sweater pockets with them and forgetting them until I hear them clunking about in the washing machine.

There are big swatches of green moss on the slopes now,

looking for all the world like the plush carpets of an old-fashioned parlor.

The jonquils are blooming by my favorite old house sites. The flowering quince has color showing along its dark stems. I saw a bit of pink on the old peach tree, and any minute little pale green fronds of fern will be uncurling.

Over on a neighbor's lake a big golden pin oak leaf that has been imprisoned under a glacé of ice floats free and reminds me of beauty past and beauty to come. A fat tadpole scoots for shelter in the weeds. A rain crow screeches at me, and I think something momentous is about to happen to the earth. That's February passing.

Spring

A flock of redbirds came early to the feeder in the back yard. From their noise I could tell it was empty. I left off watching the coffee water and ran out in my bare feet to replenish the bird seed. My feet had no sooner touched the warm, moist brick of the terrace than I wondered how I knew in advance it was going to be warm.

Some "instinct within it," as James Russell Lowell said, tells the earth it's spring and maybe it does the same for all barefooted people. Anyhow it was good to be out-of-doors shoeless.

Spiders had come in the night and spread web lace here and there on the grass under the pine trees, and the dew had silvered it. The wild plum tree by the back door, I noticed for the first time, had buds on it and the grape hyacinths a friend sent me last year were springing up all along the bed under the eaves of the house. I poked a toe under the pine needles in the bed around the little sapling on the terrace to see if I could find the special old-time white violets she sent me but I couldn't.

It could be hailing or snowing by night but for the moment it smells and feels and looks like spring. I hated to put on city clothes and leave the country. Somehow I thought going back to town would be like going back into February but I was wrong. The policeman on duty at the information desk in the rotunda of the state capitol had a vase on his desk and as I passed he picked it up and held it out for me to see. Peach blossoms. Maybe it's about to be spring everywhere.

My neighbor said she was "fretted" by March. Of all the months, she said, it's the most exasperating—neither winter nor spring but a shifty, weaving, capricious, changeling that offers you jonquils with one hand and plunges an icy dagger between your shoulder blades with the other. She does not plan to open her door or even look out her window until March has reached some kind of maturity and started behaving with proper consistency. "I hate yes-and-noism," she summed up.

All the time she talked I made noises which conveyed understanding, I hope, without conveying agreement. I'm crazy about giddy old March. You can have the stodgy "mature" months that plod along being all one thing or another. I've run my legs off trying to keep up with March and it's a privilege.

There's that sub-freezing temperature and toothy, knife-toting wind on the one hand and brilliant blue skies and goldenrod-colored sun on the other. The ice on the ground and the wind don't invite you to linger outdoors but the color of the sun and sky won't permit you to sit too long by the fire.

The miracle to me is that spring can come in spite of March. The jonquils some other woman planted at Sweet

Apple thirty or forty years ago are blooming courageously in the teeth of the wind. The ones I planted are slower . . . I wonder why.

The old-fashioned roses on the back fence have put out tiny crumpled leaves and the honeysuckle vine we left to shade the back porch from the western sun offers the same— new leaves, blue-green in color.

Six tulips have come up by the back steps and one narcissus. The house leek in the old wooden tubs by the front steps has little rosettes of green, looking like baby cabbages at the base of last year's dead stalks. The mint by the terrace is coming up and in the garden in the midst of ashes and pine straw and old grapefruit rinds I put there to nourish the soil, there are small crisp bouquets of volunteer lettuce.

The March rains overflowed lakes and ponds, washed out bridges and cut furrows in unexpected places. Water from the well is amber colored but there is plenty of it and, on the theory that it should be used fast to set the clear underground streams flowing, the washing machine runs all day.

The result may be a yellowish tinge to curtains and bedspreads but they look white blowing on the line and they smell of spring when I bring them in at dusk. At least they smell of spring until I find they are not totally dry but half frozen. Then I hang them by the oil burner to finish drying and they end up smelling slightly of kerosene.

But that's March for you and I wouldn't change it.

There's a detour on my road, where they are building a new bridge, and I've enjoyed it because it has led me to take several different routes to town. On one of these there's an old house that I've looked at often, wondered about and coveted a little bit, as I do all ramshackle, deserted country houses. Paintless, it is that soft sad gray that speaks to the country-bred of cold winter rains and harsh summer sun and poverty.

It has a tin roof that has rusted or blown off in spots, showing an old board roof underneath. Part of the rock chimney is falling down and some of the windowpanes have been replaced with tin signs.

Out back there's a serviceable-looking privy, a not at all serviceable-looking carcass of an old car, and a beautiful big pear tree that is in glorious bloom. There's a certain grace about the old house. I like its shape, a sort of north Georgia saltbox, and the way it sits, sheltered by fine old oaks.

I have often been tempted to stop and poke about it but it's too late now. I saw one morning recently that some people were moving in. Their things were strewn out in boxes and bags all along the path and the sagging front gallery was piled high with stuff. I couldn't wait to see what progress they would make settling in. I guess I visualized new panes in the windows and maybe some curtains showing, a patch on the roof and new boards on the gallery.

So far they have done nothing. Their boxes and bags and piles of clothing are still stacked high on the front gallery, looking for all the world like the curbstone collection of a family that has been evicted from a slum. There's a child's red rocker by the front steps, however, and twice a little girl has waved to me from the front door. One morning I saw an older child walking down the road with a bucket, borrowing water, I felt sure, from the nearest neighbor.

They have put up a clothesline from a post on the front porch to one of the oak trees and the clothes spread out to dry are colorful and cheerful looking.

I looked again at the old house and suddenly it seems to me that in the midst of its dilapidation it has a jolly, buoyant look. I think it is so glad to be lived in again it doesn't mind not being fixed up.

A new garden book came in the mail and right away I got hooked on a word I had noticed before—"tilth." Good tilth is what our land had before we moved in and broke it with the plow and leached it out with row crops, said this author. If you want to find soil "in good tilth" compare a handful collected in an old fence row with a handful collected in a field that has been constantly cultivated for years. The first, left alone to be enriched by leaves and grass, is highly porous, rich in organic matter and dark and crumbly. The field soil is likely to be heavier, harder and lighter in color, robbed of 20 to 50 per cent of the organic matter nature intended it to have.

Naturally I hied me to the woods to restore the tilth to my little garden patch.

For a while it was lovely work. I raked leaves under the water oak tree and watched the convocation of birds at the feeders up by the house. A mockingbird down in the woods sang, violets were blue on the bank beneath the poplar tree and the sun on my back felt like summertime.

The leaves were light and easy to haul in my garden cart but, according to my book, I was to make a kind of club sandwich of nutrients for my garden—a layer of leaves, a dusting of lime, a layer of wood's earth, a lavish seasoning of cow manure, another layer of leaves and so on until I had a concoction sufficient unto my garden needs.

The dirt down by the old sawdust pile was lovely, dark and

loose and loamy and rich with a dozen nameless fragrances. But it was heavy, too, and the briars tore at my clothes and lacerated my ankles. By the time the club sandwich in the compost bin was tall enough to be wet down with the hose I was aching in every muscle and staggering from weariness.

The tilth of my garden may be superb but if the human body has tilth mine is a mess.

This is the season when the country kitchen's window sill is likely to be its most interesting. A city kitchen window sill can retain its austere order year 'round. Suburban kitchen window sills change little, particularly if they're the new style facing the street with a wide swatch of picture-window glass above them. The colorful figurine (usually a pottery rooster) and a chaste pot of parsley or chives, if you're herb-minded, constitute its furnishings.

In the country the kitchen window sill is a catchall, a laboratory, a treasure cache. When I moved to the country I had an idea of maintaining a clean-swept window sill, particularly over the sink, so there would be no impediment to my view of the peach trees and the sweep of woods beyond.

In the dead of winter this is barely possible. Those random treasures from walks in the woods—a rock, a curiously shaped pine cone, a bit of weathered wood with moss on it, they have to be spread out somewhere for leisurely inspection and enjoyment. What better place than the kitchen window sill?

In the spring the window sill clutter thickens to the point where it all but obliterates the view. There are the moonflower seeds I started in little peat pots, hoping to have early vines on the trellis, which screens our terrace from the road.

There's the heart-shaped, copper-colored leaf I found on

the creek bank. It's not wild ginger. It's not wild geranium nor trillium. If I can keep it fresh long enough somebody will drop by and identify it. It goes in the little pitcher of water along with a sprig of an odd kind of minty-smelling plant we found on the lake banks, along with a cluster of charming white star-like flowers I knew must be something strange and exotic. (My wildflower book identified them as "great chickweed," which is disappointing but I really don't know why it should be. If a common weed is uncommonly pretty only an arrant snob would deny it a vase and a place on the window sill.)

The little wooden salad bowls take up the most space. I started dish gardens for my apartment-dwelling children but I enjoy them so much myself I am loath to give them away. A little salad bowl will hold a clump of bluets, roots and all, a tiny fern or two packed in moss, a clump of foamflowers and maybe even a rock for good measure. The whole thing lives and grows and is so interesting and spring-like I don't even notice that there's always a sifting of woods earth, a crumble or two of moss and a few dead leaves drifting over my kitchen counter.

But it is disconcerting not to be able to find a clean cup for your morning coffee because you have okra seed soaking or morning glory seed or more moonflowers soaking in everything.

Somebody has to initiate every worthwhile revival. I guess a lot of people had a hand in history's more famous one—the Renaissance that hit Europe in the fourteenth century. But I'm probably going to have to handle this one single-handedly. Why not bring back scrubbed furniture?

Not so many years ago in rural America every God-fearing, soap-making homemaker with any pretensions to cleanliness and the respect of her peers in the community, spent one morning a week, probably Saturday, scrubbing her deal table and her settin' chairs with sand and lye soap.

The beds were scrubbed too if there was any hint of bed-bug infestation. While the mattresses sunned the bedsteads got a going-over with lye water. As a result, everything in the house gleamed pale gold or silver and smelled deliciously clean.

At first blush it seems like a lot of work, all that scrubbing. But how about dusting and waxing? Talk about boring chores —and all indoors, at that.

Maybe the reason I'm so chirked up over this scrubbed furniture idea is that little cupboard I acquired some months ago. It was in a back room under a lot of stuff in Mrs. Jessie Crow's junk-antiques emporium up the road and in the dark I thought it might be something special. When I got it home it was greasy, slimy green and rat-gnawed.

I left it out in the yard for weeks and finally washed it down with boiling lye water, whereupon my relatives and friends looked it over and pronounced it a lemon—and not even an old lemon. It was poorly made of apple box pine and that durable word for country junk—"primitive"—was too good for it, they said.

Everybody advised me to haul it to the garbage dump and I almost did. Then I saw a cupboard Margie Dunn in Canton had in the kitchen of her house. She said it was in pieces when she found it in an old barn and hauled it home and every time her husband, Tommy, passed it in the yard he would laugh. When I saw it setting in her kitchen with some pretties in it, I went home and pulled my cupboard in just to see how it would look if I went to work on it with stain and shellac and beeswax.

Against the silvered old log wall the scrubbed shelves and the waggledy doors looked so at home my heart went out to the homeless little cupboard. I tried my good pewter teapot on one shelf and it looked fine. I went and got my great-grandmother's old blue steak dish and offered it to the cupboard. It accommodated it so readily I thought it must have held such country treasures before.

And the weathered, lye-scrubbed wood with the nails bleeding rust a little here and there strikes me as the most sensible "finish" I ever saw.

Lye water and sand, anyone?

The sun is hot these days and the grass is getting 'way ahead of me. Sometimes I look at that yard and wonder why we went to all the trouble to skin off the vines and underbrush and plant a lawn. There's a real grass mystique—and what's so special about grass? Thousands of people this very day are tending grass with the care and devotion normally reserved for the immortal soul. They discuss seeds and fertilizer and whether to cut high or low and when and how to water with the passion and fire of gamblers discussing horse racing.

Of course a velvety green lawn is a handsome thing but maybe we all covet one because we let ourselves fall prey to the pressure of the grass cultists. Who's to say a luxuriant patch of plantain isn't just as desirable? I looked at mine the other day and I thought, leaf for leaf, it's as handsome as that grass I've been tending.

Besides, it's useful. The common plantain, which loves my land and has determinedly cast its lot with me, is an herb which my predecessors at Sweet Apple found useful as poultices for wounds. Shakespeare even knew it. Nelson Coons, the herbal writer, recalls that Romeo asked Benvolio what plantain was good for and that worthy replied, "For your broken skin." Can you say as much for grass?

Plantain has interesting names. The Indians called it "white-man's foot" because it seemed to spring everywhere Europeans went. It is also called "way bread" and "devil's shoestring" and was once believed to be useful to draw the poison out of snake bites or to make an infusion to drink for diarrhea. In Mexico they even use it to make an ointment for sore eyes.

I ran the lawnmower over my finest patch of plantain but that's because I'm a horrid conformist. Other people like grass and I want grass. But someday when I have the courage of my convictions I'm going to fence in my plantain, cultivate it lovingly and sell pots of it to passersby at great price.

Summer

Except for birdsong and the distant crowing of a neighbor's rooster it's very quiet in the country these mornings. A young terrapin moves soundlessly across the garden path where he has been sampling green tomatoes. A small brown rabbit, caught pilfering the ruby lettuce, sits motionless and wide-eyed.

Brownie, who is really Quinton Johnson's hound but does a bit of volunteer watchdogging for me, comes up from the woods with his two adopted charges, a brace of soft-muzzled, big-footed young beagles, capering behind him. They stop when they see me drinking my coffee on the terrace and back up shyly but are emboldened to come closer when they observe that Brownie is not afraid to pause beside my rocker and let me pat his head.

The sun's emergence from the pine woods is the signal for the sounds of June to begin, crickets and katydids and July flies, bees humming about the peach trees. A green apple falls with a soft plop, a lizard comes out from under the house and scuds across the gray bark of the trellis with a dry whispery sound.

My garden is late with kitchen produce but early with opulent, rich-looking weeds. The catnip plant I left in the middle of one plot, hoping it would repel whatever insects specialize in eggplant, is a beautiful buxom, silver-green bouquet of minty fragrance. (Mrs. Crow says this same catnip was "the saving of the settlemint" years ago when winter colds and pneumonia struck and doctors and drug stores were far away.) It didn't save my eggplants, however, because they are drawnwork and thread lace.

The lowly portulaca plants I stuck in the cracks of the rock retaining wall, just because they were available, open their flowers to the sun—flamboyant, many-petaled, jewel-toned blooms that reproach me for my indifference to them.

Queen Anne's lace has popped up in all the flowerbeds and I haven't the heart to pull it up. It's really prettier and more vigorous than any of the boughten plants I have brought in and pampered.

The roadsides are bountiful with a gratuitous harvest—wild plums as bright as Christmas tree baubles, blackberries ripening fast, an amber tide of old-fashioned day lilies, Sweet Williams, black-eyed Susans, New Jersey tea, and the orange flame of butterfly bush.

These are the longest days of the year, these June days—but not long enough. You can't have too much June, I say.

Now I'm beginning to understand Thoreau's preoccupation with Walden Pond. A body of water can be a very engrossing thing. Jack is acquiring what has become wonderfully stylish in our countryside—a lake. And all of us who gave him a hand in the building thereof have watched each new development as avidly as city people kibbitz the erection of a skyscraper.

From the moment he started putting out stakes to mark the boundaries of the proposed lake, neighbors from all sides began trudging over the site.

The soil conservation specialists came and recommended and the old hands amongst us argued with them over the merits of this place for the dam as against that place.

The time came to cut the trees and I tried to stay away because I couldn't bear to see the fallen trunks of the big oaks and beeches or the carnage in dogwoods, maples and sourwoods. But as soon as the power-saw crews departed I was one of the eagerest beavers on the spot, mooching my share of logs for the fireplace. Then the earth-moving machines came in and every man and boy in the settlement took up his post on the hillside to watch or to lend a hand at brush hauling and burning.

The day the great raw red clay dam was finished and they put the stopper in the drain and began to let the basin fill up we were all there, making guesses as to how long before we could swim or fish.

In spite of the dry weather the lake has filled rapidly and now we go daily to place twigs on the bank to mark the water's rise. Sometimes it's late when we get there and the lake is a dark mirror full of reflections but there's nothing lonely or brooding about this new body of water. To my surprise, it ripples with life and noise.

The frogs must have gotten the word first that there was a new lake a-building because I think they have assembled from as far away as Crabapple, Birmingham Community and Hickory Flat. They set up their music stands on the banks every evening and make a raucous chorus that you can hear for miles around. We took a flashlight one night and were astonished to find that one bull-voiced fellow was a little spotted frog not much bigger than your thumb.

Crickets have joined them. Spring lizards luxuriate in the still water along the bank. Little waterbugs skim over the surface, pulling the fabric of the lake after them in small accordion pleats, and late-flying birds swoop down for a bedtime dip or snack. Sometimes we linger long moments, listening and watching, awed by the miracle of water and its attraction for all life.

"Something there is that doesn't love a wall," wrote that sharp and canny old countryman Mr. Robert Frost. Although you sense that Mr. Frost himself was at one with nature in that view and I would hesitate to disagree with the sage of Vermont about most things, I must confess something there is that does love a wall. Me. Old stone walls and country fences have a sensible grace and symmetry that please me even as Mr. Frost's poems do. I admire them for many reasons having nothing to do with keeping anything in or keeping anything out.

Fences are fine for climbing when you want to see if somebody's coming or to watch a sunset. They hold roses and other vines handily. They add a certain variety and character to the landscape. Besides all that, they are, on some occasions, great fun to build.

Our first fence at Sweet Apple was made up of poles which we got by tearing down an old abandoned peeled pole barn over on Roy Morgan's land. We made a day of it one Saturday, taking picnic baskets and coolers, and when the barn was dismantled and the sound poles loaded on the truck, we went blackberrying.

The fence, posts and two runs of poles, lasted until we lucked into an old zigzag chestnut rail fence from Mr. Henry Troutman's place over near Upper Hembree. Mister Henry, a handsome, distinguished Atlanta lawyer, now in his eighties, and his wife, Miss Mag, used to spend their summers over on Elkin Road in an old country house with a lake in its front yard and a creek in its back yard. But recently they've been staying in the city mostly. When we heard the county was going to widen and pave the road past their country house and that the rail fence might have to be moved, I asked Mister Henry if he would consider selling it to me.

He came out one Saturday to see if Sweet Apple was "fitten" for his fence, toured the premises and said promptly, "I never saw a more fitten place for that rail fence. You need it and I'm going to give it to you—the corncrib, too, if you can get it moved."

So now every weekend that I can mobilize work crews we haul rails and rocks—rocks to construct a foundation for the corncrib.

My mother, Muv, has watched the removal of the fence from Mister Henry's property to mine with some trepidation.

"Who," she asked, "is going to lay the worm?"

The worm, it seems, is the first line of rails and they must be laid with great precision. You have to mark off the place where the points will come and drive stobs and put up strings and all like that. It was my idea to let the fence sort of meander across the front of my estate any way it wanted to, avoiding pine and dogwood where I wanted to keep them and generally adapting itself to the existing terrain.

That's not the way with rail fences, says Muv. Mine and the birds' cherished tangle of goldenrod and Queen Anne's

lace and maypop vines by the road must go. Roses pull a
fence down. Hollyhocks grow too tall. What I need, says Muv,
is phlox—low-growing phlox in all the fence corners. It will
be too late to plant it by the time we get all the rails moved
and the fence assembled but I guess it's settled that I'll plant
phlox. I wouldn't want to do anything that wasn't fitten.

There's a splendid new edifice in my back yard—Mister
Henry's 134-year-old corncrib. Jack and Quinton Johnson dismantled and moved it one Saturday and now Quinton and
another carpenter have reassembled it, setting the notched
logs straight and true. We've put a window in the opening
where the farmers used to throw in their ears of corn from
the wagon and cut a door in the other side. This was painful
for me, seeing the saw cut through those lovely old logs, but
if I'm going to use it for a workroom, as I hope, I really must
have a door.

Quinton made me some bookshelves and a door from old
boards but we had to use new boards to put over the cracks
between the logs and that old problem, how to match those
artists, time and the weather, arose again. The outside was
grayish like Sweet Apple cabin but the inside was something
entirely different.

I had imagined it too was a soft silvery gray but the heart
of old chestnut logs, sheltered from the weather and embrac-
ing, for over a hundred years, corn, sometimes hay and potatoes, and occasionally a litter of coon hounds, takes on a
lovely color. It was both golden and rose. Margie Dunn said
"mud colored" and she meant not dirty dirt but the good earth
in all the wonderful rich range of colors that Georgia's soil
comes in. I've been mixing mudpies and I think I'm on the

right track: yellowish clay, pinked up a bit with the deep rose clay, which nurtured cotton and corn and peaches and pumpkins so well for centuries, mixed with water and grayed a little with wood ashes. Rub it on with a rag and it is a near match.

There comes a time in the country when you just have to take the bull by the horns and haul off those bottles and cans. I put it off as long as I can and I don't know why because it's always a pleasant trip. Our neighbors, Dr. and Mrs. Bernard Wolff, have offered us the ultimate in hospitality— an invitation to dump in a ravine by the edge of their pasture.

We have contributed substantially to the hideous litter, which is slowly filling up the washed-out earth, and I am always waylaid by retrieving something I shouldn't have thrown away or hauling home something somebody else threw away. (A wooden soft-drink case with all its little partitions made a marvelous nail box for the workbench and once we found a perfectly splendid minnow trap.) In contrast to the garbage the prettiest flowers bloom along that bank and I always ride to the dump with a flower book open beside me on the seat.

The other day I found a strange white bloom which must be Culver's root or Veronicastrum Virginicum. It fits Jean Hersey's description. (White. Two to seven feet. Flowers at top of stalk bend like kittens' tails. Blooms in summer in meadows and woodlands. May pick.)

There's a clump of Turk's-cap lilies, extremely elegant and exotic looking. I would have thought them fugitives from some old-time garden except that I have Miss Hersey's word that they are wild. She says monarch butterflies depend on the Turk's-cap lily as a source of nectar and adds: "Blooms summer, everywhere. Don't pick."

Guiltily, I took one bloom and sneaked home with it, feeling elated and larcenous and not a bit like a lady who had merely been to dump the garbage.

Missionaries and diplomats are sure to have known for centuries what I've just learned about making converts. That is, the same set of aims and ideals won't motivate every Tom, Dick and Harry. It took the advent of the fishing season, for instance, for me to convert my children to my program of conserving and using the kitchen garbage.

They've laughed at "Mama's Garbage Game," the sorting of piles labeled: 1. Burn. 2. Haul. 3. Bury. Eggshells and coffee grounds and potato peels and grapefruit rinds are not dear to their hearts, as they are to mine.

But the other day I found Jimmy and Edward digging for fish bait in my compost pile. Every time the shovel turned up a load of dark loamy soil, tastefully laced with pine straw, oak leaves and rotten potatoes, there would be a wriggling handful of fat earthworms. I thought I saw the chance to advance the cause of organic gardening and I spoke of how this fine earthwormy soil was matchless for growing geraniums and tomatoes and beans and everything.

They weren't listening. They were scooping up worms and putting them in bait cans as fast as they could. But I did hear them say, as they headed for the lake, that they planned to use any worms that were left over to stock compost piles of their own in the city.

Fishing relaxes some people but I prefer fish watching.

That way you don't have to fool with lines and bait and all that stuff. By the time you have a pole properly rigged and baited, if you haven't caught the hook in your own clothes, hair or hide, you have hooked somebody else, snagged a bush or caught a fish.

And if you have a fish there's a decision over keeping him. We don't keep bass under a pound for the health of the herd, I think. Any bream you catch is a keeper but it's pointless unless you're going to take home a mess. So you have all that to decide, which isn't restful at all.

Much to be preferred, to my notion, is fish watching. You can sit empty-handed on a ferny bank up under the shade of a fragrant spice bush or sourwood and let your tired mind and spirit sink into the clear green waters of the lake where bright-scaled fish dart and play.

Together they put on an underwater tableau which is completely restful. In fact, after I had watched the fish for twenty minutes the other day, lifting my eyes occasionally to admire a cloud or a tree branch, I was so at peace with the world that I could contemplate the passage—twenty or thirty feet away —of a long black snake in pursuit of a frog. Ordinarily I would have fled from the scene quaking but fish watching gives you a kind of tranquil objectivity, I guess.

Miss Pal sent me word the other day that she wanted to see me "first chance" and as soon as I could find the time and weather right for negotiating the road to her cabin I obeyed the summons. She was annoyed, it turned out, because some neighbor who had come to have her conjure off a virulent case of poison ivy told her I had written of being wakeful and "worrisome" in the night.

I told her whatever it was had passed and I wasn't fretting over anything at the moment. It was just some run-of-the-mill, ordinary worry, I suggested, like everybody has.

Miss Pal was scraping new potatoes for her dinner and she gouged out a couple of potato eyes with an unwonted fierceness.

Worry, she said, is a sign of weak-mindedness and she had surely thought better of me.

"I want to tell you about worry," she went on. "Hit's agin God and nature. Hit frets your sleep, frays your appetite, spiles your digestion, sours your disposition and is the ruination of mind and health.

"The Lord God," she went on, "never intended His creatures to waste their time and stren'th in ways that don't hep nothing. Ask yourself can you do something to hep. If you can, git at it. If you cain't, roll over, say your prayers and go back to sleep."

Miss Pal admitted that she used to worry.

"I used to dip snuff and talk about the neighbors, too. I've give up all three and ast the Lord to forgive me. You can do the same."

I'm trying. So far snuff's the only thing I've completely renounced.

These are strenuous days in the country. Gardens are at that stage where something is ripening every minute. Artie Cox, whose homemade butter and buttermilk are without peer, keeps the kind of kitchen you like to think of when you're hungry—shiningly clean, fragrant and comfortable. Doors open in summer to a breeze that smells of green grass and flowers.

The other day I dropped by with Julia and Louise, who had come up from the coast for a visit, to pick up a jug of buttermilk. She saw us coming and called hospitably from the window: "Come in but don't look at a thing, please!"

We did go in and the kitchen looked fine to us but we understood her dilemma. She was in the midst of canning beans. The pressure cooker was about to go off. She had a cake due out of the oven. Her electric churn had grown over-zealous and started spewing buttermilk all over the floor. She was working one mound of butter—and the telephone rang.

It was enough to send a lesser woman into the city to spend the afternoon sitting in an air-conditioned movie looking at a picture about rich adventuresses or something. But Miss Artie is a conscientious and competent housekeeper and I feel sure she worked herself out of her dilemma before long.

She had to. I noticed, as I passed, that more beans were ready for picking in her garden, tomatoes are ripening and all that cabbage . . . gracious, she had to get a grip on herself and start putting down sauerkraut soon.

When your garden patch is no bigger than mine—about the size of a hearth rug—you don't need to plant corn, says Doc. You might as well stop at a supermarket or a roadside stand on the way home from town and buy corn grown by somebody else.

It goes hard with me to differ with Doc but I planted three six-foot rows of corn and I think Doc is reconciled because of the sheer freakishness of my crop. You never saw such corn.

I should have thinned it but every little emerald blade looked so smart and dauncy marching along there in the dark red earth I just shoveled some more cow manure along the rows and left them to grow cheek by jowl. Every single blade took off and grew like Jack's beanstalk and now we have the spectacle of a gorgeous, if limited, thicket of corn taller than any elephant's eye you ever saw.

Such refulgent foliage may not "make," my neighbors say, and if it does produce corn I'll need the hook and ladder company of the Roswell Fire Department to help me harvest it.

But I cherish that corn for esthetic reasons. It is prettier than a green taffeta ball gown and it sounds about the same. On a moonlight night I wander out to the wagon seat under the apple tree and listen to that corn growing.

It shimmers and ripples like dark green water. There's music in its growing and if it doesn't "make"—shoot, roas'n' ears with all that country butter dripping from them are fattening anyhow.

The garden is at its productive best now and by galloping at full tilt we can harvest the tomatoes, great green bell peppers and beans before the weeds take them. The okra really gives you a race for your money. You have to cut it every single day or those tender little pods that we enjoy boiling whole and dipping in lemon juice and butter will be big pods and too tough to eat whole.

Pleasure in our home-grown vegetables is slightly marred for Muv, however, because of the sad situation with corn meal. Muv feels about corn meal the way some people feel about wine. The wine bibber, tasting and smelling, seeking a "bouquet," turning his glass between his fingers in the light, examining the color of the wine and then making his pronouncement as to the very region, the exact vineyard in

France where it grew, hasn't a thing on Muv and corn meal.

She, too, uses all her senses on meal, rubbing it between her fingers for texture, shaking out a little the better to see the color, smelling for freshness and tasting for whatever it is you taste in raw meal.

And I have it on Muv's authority that the world is in a bad way for decent meal.

"Bought meal!" she scoffed when she saw the package in my cupboard. "Honey, have you come to this?" She read the label and gave me that dark, bright-eyed glance which said as plain as words that her own flesh and blood was betraying her. "Self-rising!" She threw the word at me as if it were a moral indictment.

I promised her that we would go up to Aubrey Chadwick's store on Saturday morning and remedy the meal situation. Chadwick's store is on the site of an old grist mill and I felt sure Aubrey had a proper feeling about corn meal. But it turned out that his shelves held only what Muv dismissed scornfully as "Mixes and 'additive' stuff!"

"You don't need anything in meal except good corn properly ground," she told him.

He was apologetic. He said he had made arrangements with one of the neighbors to get some good corn and get it ground and it should be in within a few days.

"We're having beans and corn and okra for supper," Muv said severely. "How can we wait?"

Then I had an inspiration. Mr. and Mrs. Lum Crow had mentioned having to take their corn to mill. Maybe they would lend us some meal.

We went by their house and while Mrs. Crow got the meal

Mr. Crow showed us his corn patch—"roas'n' ears" for now and "bread corn" coming on.

Muv was soothed and reassured only temporarily. It alarms her to think that corn bread eaters the world over haven't Mr. and Mrs. Crow to borrow from and are at the mercy of those who slip baking powder and salt and maybe worse into honest meal.

Their nesting time past, August is the season for boldness among my wild neighbors in the country.

The rabbits come out at twilight and with great insouciance sit under the tents of drying weeds and sun-blistered tomatoes in my garden and nibble the tender underleaves of gone-to-seed lettuce.

The quail who live in the weeds under the rail fence take their children for a stroll, marshaling them along with the serene pride of a country family going to Sunday meeting.

The cardinals, apparently irritated with me for letting the bird seed run out, even in this season of opulence in woods and field, come up on the back steps and peck at the green corn I have temporarily left there.

In this season of green corn, when the ironweed is just coming out along the roadsides and the first plumes of joe-pye weed are turning purple down by the creek bank, it's inconceivable that winter will ever come. Country fairs are beginning, family reunions are at their peak. The children run about barefoot with never a thought of the painful business of school shoes coming up.

But the bees seem to me to be tackling the mint bed with renewed vigor. Great floppy butterflies dreamily sail the sunlit morning air and the July flies strum away in the trees. In fact, the whole sound of the days and early evenings is a riper, deeper sound of cricket and frog and birdsong. The light tentative tunes of the spring and early summer have matured. The mourning dove and whippoorwill are surer of themselves, the frogs croak with undeniable authority.

Of course the days are hotter than they ever have been but sometimes at bedtime or in the early morning there's a sharp edge of coolness in the air. And the other day when I turned out of the driveway I noticed Queen Anne's lace and the little purple heal-all flowers were already dried arrangements. For a minute I could see them as they were last February, rimed with frost.

Summer, I fear, is reaching the end of her tether. In no time at all this lovely emerald and gold season, which smells of peaches and grapes ripening, will be an old has-been.

Fall

Of all the months September is the one for sitting in the shade and feeling the earth turn or walking in the wheat-colored sunlight and watching it glisten.

There's not enough time to spend out-of-doors in September. Friends who are in the kitchen canning or poking about closets pulling out bedding to sun and assessing the moth damage to winter clothes have my greatest admiration. But I cannot copy them because I always have a feeling that this day, this perfect September day, will never come again and I'd better get outside and look at it.

It was a right accomplishing week—the vacation I took at home. We cleared out the hollow where all the leftover lumber and tin from rebuilding the cabin has been stacked.

Then there was the day Mitch Suttles, the rock mason of local renown, came to work on the chimney. The first year we went through the winter with a sheet of tin nailed in the chimney corner outside and nubbins of wood and rock wool insulation chinking the chimney cracks inside. The slightest breeze stirred the rock wool and let in both daylight and cold air.

This year I determined that in a land where beautiful field stones abound I would have my chimney shored up if I had to do it myself. Fortunately for the chimney, Mr. Suttles had some time to spare me.

Mitch Suttles is a giant of a man—six feet, five inches tall and with girth to match—and he has been building chimneys and rock walls and houses all over north Georgia since he was a little shirttail boy not even in his teens. Serving fifty-eight months with the army overseas kept him from getting cocky about a calling in which he enjoys considerable prestige hereabouts.

"I'm not a rock mason," he said. "We haven't got any rock masons in this country. I found that out after I saw the rock work in Italy. You talk about beautiful masonry, that's where they got it!"

But he does have one pretension. His chimneys don't smoke. At least I hope they don't. I sure don't feel like moving those big slabs of granite he stuck up over the air holes around my hearth if there should be anything wrong with my fireplace's "draw" now.

There's a bumper crop of young lizards and toad frogs this fall. Every time I pass the woodpile a whole passel of baby lizards of fingerling size go skittering out of my path and into my winter supply of fireplace wood.

Every time I take a cup of coffee and go out on the rock stoop and watch the sunset or the wind stirring around in the pine thicket across the road, a gaggle of little spotted frogs plummets out of somewhere to make hop toad passes at my feet. The other day, just as I gained the door, a young lizard darted ahead of me and it suddenly occurred to me we were both heading for the same place: inside my house. Now I don't fear lizards or anything like that but it doesn't cheer me to think that they might be planning to move indoors for the winter and although it isn't cold, winter can't be far away.

Goldenrod has lifted its mustardy plumes along the road. Pokeberries are purple by the kitchen wall where I left a plant, thinking it as decorative as a flower. Ironweed and joe-pye weed and black-eyed Susans are holding carnival in old vacant fields. Down in the woods the sourwood and black gums are turning red and the sumac is burgundy velvet. The poplars have as many gold leaves on them as green, and the black walnuts are losing their leaves already, becoming funny picture-book trees hung with the lime green fruit of their nuts.

The heat of midday doesn't fool Muv. It is but the last fling of summer, and she celebrates what she knows is the coming of fall by having a big pot of backbone and rice simmering on the back of the stove when we come in from work.

To Muv the greatest trouble that can come to an older person is the loss of home. Illness and even death are the natural portion of the elderly and therefore supportable, but to have to give up one's home before that final departure is a real tragedy. Our cousin, Sister, approaching her eightieth birthday, reached that point. She could not care for herself and it was decided that she would sell her house and go to a nursing home. I went with Muv to see her.

Sister didn't need any help from us. The jolly, compassionate woman who runs the nursing home had taken care of much of the packing and good friends had rallied 'round to help her get the best possible price for her little house. But she seemed glad of our presence as we visited and drank coffee in the front room of the nursing home. She looked more fragile, a little slower of movement. But her cotton print dress with the frills at the neck was fresh and crisp and she made the same merry faces as she referred to herself and Muv as "us girls."

We were ready to go before she suggested driving over to her little house with the "For Sale" sign in the yard.

Although it was warm and sunny outside, the house was chilly and shadowy inside, and Sister stood a moment looking at the packing boxes by the door, the empty shelves and the blank television set. Then she began to pick up things left at random here and there.

The old carnival glass sugar bowl and spoon holder which have occupied the center of her dining-room table as long as I can remember caught the light in their iridescent, grape-patterned depths and Sister picked them up.

"Take these home with you," she said to me. "I'll never use them again. You ought to have them in the country."

Then she remembered that there had been a cream pitcher with them and she started worrying and opening and closing cupboard doors. Was it packed away or did she break it years ago? She couldn't remember and it bothered her so she kept moving restlessly from room to room, looking. Her eye fell on an old blue crockery pitcher and she handed it to me. A gilt-framed tinted photograph of a simpering woman playing a harp leaned against the wall and she brushed it with her fingers and stood a moment looking at it.

"Ma came to stay with me in Waycross when Roy was born," she said. "She bought that picture for my parlor. You take it—I reckon it's an antique—Roy will be fifty-five his next birthday."

Suddenly I didn't want any more. I wanted to get out in the sunshine and head home. I signaled to Muv and we prepared to leave. And then I turned to see Sister holding in her outstretched hand a little glass bottle with a gold-edged rim.

"You can use it for a bud vase," she said. "It's really a hatpin holder I got on the Christmas tree at Nichols, Georgia, when I was fifteen years old. But you don't need hatpin holders now, do you?"

It wasn't a sad question but for some reason it was enough. We put our arms around each other and cried together.

When I am an old lady with lots of time to spend in the research department of the public library there are a lot of historical questions I hope to look into. For instance, to whom are we indebted for the apparently fixed and immutable notion that spider webs are undesirable things to have around a house?

I have an idea that it was some neurotic ninny of a cave woman who either wanted her hole in the cliff to be the flossiest one in the area or was so loaded with hostilities toward her fellow creatures that all she knew to do was to lay about her with a broom, batting down anything smaller than she was.

The marvel is that in this enlightened twentieth century thousands of men and women the world over expend thousands of valuable hours following her example, destroying what they could not by the wildest stretch of the imagination recreate themselves, the delicate gossamer web of their neighbor, the spider.

If we had to import spiders and plan special crops to feed them and build them workrooms to shelter them from the cold and heat, we'd hail each new web they made with glad and admiring cries. We'd rearrange our rooms to show off an especially fine specimen of the spider's art and contrive ways to preserve it.

The other day, poking about with a broom, I absently started to swipe at a web stretched across the bottom of the little three-legged stool Margaret and Buster Farran gave me to set by the fireplace. I tilted the stool and sunlight pouring in the window glinted on the web and I really saw it for the first time—a beautiful, perfect job of work, lovingly rounded and meticulously fastened to the smooth pine wood of the stool.

A small gray spider sat in the middle of it, a modest, unassuming little housewife, looking out from her own threshold. I thought of a line by Pope, "The spider's touch, how exquisitely fine!" and I put the stool back and took my broom elsewhere.

Traffic on our little dirt road and the telephone interfered with the Sunday afternoon nap I was bent on taking so I gave up and put on a robe and was puttering about the back steps drinking a cup of coffee when I saw Mr. Lum Crow swinging down the road. His usual free, Indian-like movement was a little hampered by something he was carrying under one arm.

"What you got there, Mr. Crow?" I called.

"Got my racket box," he said. And held up his old Bruno banjo for me to see.

"My brother, Everett, come over for dinner and brought his fiddle and we thought we'd play some together but it didn't amount to much."

I smiled at Mr. Crow's modest statement. He never permits himself an extravagant utterance or an exaggeration. If his jam session with his fiddling brother had wound up like the Newport Jazz Festival with fighting in the streets Mr. Crow would have dealt with it in very temperate terms.

As always, Mr. Crow inspected our newest project, putting hand-rived white oak boards on the roof of the little utility house. He said he heard I was out of boards and he had his froe and could rive me some if we could just find a suitable "board tree." We talked about the dimensions of good board trees for a time, and then he said he'd play me a tune before he had to go home and put out some corn to his fattening hog, known simply as Pig.

We pulled up chairs on the terrace and my neighbor cradled his banjo in his arms.

"Had this thing fifty-eight years," he remarked as he tuned it.

Then he started playing. First there was "Soldier's Joy."

"Reckon that one is about two hundred years old," Mr. Crow explained when the last lively note was still.

After that he played, "I'm Gonna Leave This Old Place," followed by "Finger Ring." Mr. Crow professes not to be a singer but now and then the music will take hold of him and in a firm, true voice he'll give you a lyric or two. I especially liked "Finger Ring" and the verses which ran something like this:

My old hound dog has left me;
I wish they'd bring him back.
Chased the big hogs over the fence
And the little ones through the crack.

Asked that girl to marry me.
This is what she said:
Yes, yes, I'll marry you . . .
When everybody else is dead.

We laughed over the ways of a choosy woman and he played on a few minutes. The sun was gone and it was gray and cool on the terrace. That reminded Mr. Crow of Pig's needs and he stood up and swung his racket box over his shoulder.

A Sunday afternoon nap is well lost for such a Sunday afternoon concert.

As long as I can remember one of the delights of the first wintry day of the year was coming home from school to find a pot of vegetable soup simmering on the back of the stove. That soup started in November—or October, if it was cold enough—and, with certain artistic additions and subtractions, lasted almost till spring, always getting better.

When Muv came to visit at Sweet Apple a week or so ago we had one of those sudden cold days and we both thought simultaneously of soup. Not a casual soup out of a can or a package, although they are nourishing and tasty and handy to have, but a start-with-the-bone, lovingly assembled poetry of a soup.

Fortunately for our soup-making rite Chadwick's is the kind of country store where they *give* you soup bones. None of this weighing and wrapping in cellophane and stamping with a price roughly equivalent to a sirloin steak for them.

You say to the young butcher, "Alonzo, have you a good knuckle bone for me today?"

And Alonzo retires to the cold-storage room and emerges with half a cow, sets it down on the block and with a profligate hand chops you off a great meaty joint. This, simmered all day long, gives forth gelatin, marrow, flavor and an aroma that reaches out into the cold air and brings hunters, tramps and random motorists to the door.

After a day of simmering, the bones are lifted out, stripped of any bit of lean meat that hasn't cooked off, and along with most of the suet, bestowed on Brownie. Then begins the gradual addition of goodies to the broth. I fling what I have into the pot. Not my mother, Muv. She has a timetable.

Carrots and onions first—they take a lot of cooking. Snap beans at some time when the broth is cool. (Never start snap beans in hot water.) She will use corn freshly cut off the cob but canned corn never. ("Clouds the broth and the soup doesn't keep as well.") Potatoes and tomatoes go in and sometimes a handful of spaghetti or rice and after that I lose track.

The first day of the soup nobody can stay out of the kitchen. The young folks come in from cutting wood or tramping through the woods to the lake and lift the lid on the big pot and inquire if we need them to taste the soup for us. Toward mid-afternoon they don't ask but get out mugs and cups and ladle out a little "to see what it needs."

Little hot corn cakes go with the maiden meal of the season's first pot of vegetable soup, but after that French bread with sweet butter from Artie Cox's cows suffices. (With second- or third-day soup you don't have to make a ceremony of stirring and browning those little baby hoecakes. Ceremonies are for first days.)

If William Makepeace Thackeray had ever pulled up a chair to a good slow-burning oak log and dipped a spoon into Muv's vegetable soup, he would have written a poem far better than his "Ballad of Bouillabaisse."

As it is, some of his paean to that lovely seafood conglomeration applies to Muv's soup:

> Indeed, a rich and savoury stew 'tis;
> And true philosophers, methinks,
> Who love all sorts of natural beauties,
> Should love good victuals and good drinks.

It being November, Muv had to go home to vote. She'll be over at the community house when the polls open, operating on some private, unproven theory that the early voter gets the victory. I'm just glad for her neighbors that the Australian ballot is used and Muv can never be sure how they vote because she takes her politics hard.

In a way I'm glad politics is still a fighting matter with Muv because in other areas she's not as lionhearted as she used to be.

When she comes to Sweet Apple she starts looking immediately for locks on the doors. Such fasteners as we have seem effective enough to me. Tom Stover, a mountain friend, made me a wooden latch for the front door that has a hickory spring which slides a hickory bolt into place when the door is shut. The kitchen door has a leather thong for a latch string and when you pull in the latch string that says plainly enough to all visitors, burglars and all, that you're not receiving.

"Pshaw," said Muv, "I won't sleep a wink in such a place! I'm going to get Quinton Johnson to put bars across the door this very day—stout hickory ones, set in iron."

It wasn't convenient for Mr. Johnson to get to that job right away and it worried Muv some but she did sleep—thirty minutes at a time. Every half hour she would sit bolt upright in bed and whisper hoarsely: "What's that? Turn on the outside lights . . . I hear something!"

Now the leaves are gone except for a few tattered brown flags defiantly hoisted to the wind by the maples and the oaks. The grass has been touched by frost and is the restful winter brown that I like fully as well as summer's bright green.

The sunsets and sunrises are daily shows of breath-taking splendor. And in between are the moonlit nights and the days when the sky, like a baby's face, reflects every mood both stormy and benign.

It's hard to stay in bed these mornings. If you can beat the sun up you have a little time of day when it is both morning and night. To the east beyond the pines there day waits in the wings in robes of rose and gold ready to make her entrance. And to the west in a pure silver sky the moon hovers, reluctant to bow out.

These mornings my volunteer watchdog, Brownie, has urgent errands elsewhere. The soft bed I made for him out of an old bedspread and a motheaten wool dress by the back door is cold.

I caught the sound of his voice mingled with others baying on a far hill during the night and he won't return until mid-morning probably. Then dew-wet and weary he will come trotting up from the woods holding his tail like a coiled steel spring and baring his teeth in one of his curious wolf-like smiles.

I'm not sure what Brownie pursues. He's not the kind of hunter to bring anything home. But whatever it is, the exuberance of the chase seems to be enough for him.

Sometimes I envy Brownie his freeness to roam the hills and valleys at night, to feel the rough frosty grass beneath his feet and smell all the dark pungent perfume of fallen leaves, decaying woods and the weedy scents of rabbit tobacco and horsemint. He can wade creeks and pause and drink if he wants to. He can stop and rest on a hilltop and look at the sky for long moments.

Brownie is unafraid of his night world. A moving shadow to him is not a menace but a challenge. He rushes out to meet it, to bark it down and chase it under a log or up a tree.

It's a puny thing to be a fearful, housebound woman—to worry about snakes and brambles that pull at your clothes and scrape your skin, to avoid wet feet and catching a cold.

Sometimes when I stand in the back door in the morning watching the sun come up and the moon go down I think of this with a sense of loss and regret. It's so wasteful to live in a world you don't see.

And then I go in the house and latch the door and turn up the furnace and put the coffee on.

Christmas

Christmas is a season all to itself at Sweet Apple—maybe technically winter but a very special chunk of winter filled with special tasks and excitement. We're tireder than usual, busier than usual and, I believe, happier than usual.

We make monumental plans for food and decorations and loving-hands-at-home gifts, most of which gang oft a-gley. Nothing ever seems to get finished. The cabin is jammed with company, the children and their children and friends. Cots and rollaway beds fill the living room and if you're not careful when you move around at night you'll stumble over a body on the floor.

The fire burns late on the hearth, the air is redolent of pine, candlewax and scorched popcorn. And the old pump organ which Doc's sister, Betty, turned over to me when she moved to a city apartment, is seldom silent.

Everybody who can come home does but of course with grown-up children there are sometimes absences. The first Christmas I was in Sweet Apple cabin Susan and Edward were at Fort Benning. They came for a weekend before Christmas, bringing Muv with them, and received a most un-Christmasy reception. The pipes had frozen, every dish in the house stood on the counter gray with congealed grease, the plumbing didn't function and my old car decided to give up the ghost.

Jimmy was at home then. (He was to marry and move back to town a year and a half later.) We rode to our jobs with Jack and since one of us always seemed to have to work late, it was often close to midnight when we got back to the country.

We had not expected Susan, Edward, baby John and Muv the night they came. We thought they would arrive the next day and we'd have time to thaw the pipes, wash the dishes and get things a bit Christmasy. But we arrived to find Susan and the baby huddled by the hearth where Edward struggled to make a fire with wet wood. Muv with her wool bathrobe on over her clothes was stuffing toilet paper into the cracks of the front door with a pair of eyebrow tweezers.

It took a while. Jack went under the house with a blow torch to tackle the pipes. Jimmy started moving lumber piles looking for dry wood for fire-starting and I hastily threw a sheet over the rocker I was antiquing for Susan's Christmas present, set up the baby bed for John, made cocoa and cheese toast all around and the dirty, disorderly, cold little cabin was soon warm and full of laughter and talk and as Christmasy as it could be.

Mary and Cricket have been away several Christmases, a couple of times at army bases and recently in California, where they went to live. And although I'm reconciled, there's always a pre-Christmas sinking spell when I yearn to have them all under one roof again.

It's the little things that make you miss people. This is true when they die and it's also true when they simply go away. A joke, the shape of branches against the sky, a scrap of music, the familiar slant of writing on an envelope . . . these things set off a siege of loneliness or yearning when you least expect it, when, in fact, you've come to consider yourself immune. It was a bird's nest, soft and compact and perfect, in a tangle of honeysuckle vine that set me to missing Susan the first Christmas she was away.

Some people take Christmas. Others make it. Susan is the one in our family who makes it. She's the one all of us consult about presents for others. She's in on every gift-wrapped conspiracy and is usually the one to do the wrapping. She is an inspired and indefatigable shopper and we all load her down with our errands.

The Christmas she was away the others were at home and I thought I was rejoicing in her reports on her first efforts to make fruitcake, her first Santa Claus shopping for a child of her own and all the things she was doing to make a drab army housing apartment holidayish.

There was no ache in missing her until I cut through the woods at the edge of the yard to collect some Scotch pine branches with their lovely little brown cones. There in the honeysuckle was the bird's nest—so soft and perfect and empty.

I picked it up carefully, thinking about the birds that had flown and sort of absently wondering if I could do something Christmasy with it when I heard myself saying Susan's name aloud.

One thing about a cold December afternoon, moisture in your eyes could be whipped there by the wind.

The fact that Muv always arrives for her Christmas visit with a full quota of holiday cakes beautifully browned or iced, as the case may be, without a crumb out of place, is an indication to me of some pioneer spirit. I believe she could have journeyed across the continent fighting off the Indians with a melodeon tied to the back of her covered wagon and arrive without a single key out of kilter.

Muv feels strongly about nearly everything but when she undertakes Christmas cakes she becomes a martinet. Her neighbors, realizing that Atlanta is a big metropolitan center with a full complement of fine bakeries, have suggested on one or more occasions that it isn't necessary for Muv to make her Christmas visit armed to the nines with cakes.

"Bakery cakes!" sniffs Muv. "Chalk and sugar."

And she preheats her oven and gets out her special cake pans, the ones she uses for absolutely nothing else and will not even lend. (To keep from hurting her neighbors' feelings she maintains a separate collection of cake pans to lend. These are not kept as bright and untarnished as her private stock.)

Then I don't know what all goes on in her kitchen in Alford except that she considers it a poor "do" if she isn't feeling strong enough to do all the beating by hand and has to rely on an electric mixer.

"I can tell an electrically mixed cake," she maintains. "The texture is all wrong. If you haven't got the gumption to beat a cake yourself you shouldn't call yourself making a cake."

(I never have confessed this to Muv but I not only can't tell if it's a hand-beaten cake but I stoop to use cake mixes and have been known to eat boughten cake with some pleasure.)

When her cakes are ready Muv has to fight negativism in

the members of her "crowd"—ladies named Miss Minnie, Miss Josie, Miss Pearl, all of ripe years and experience and an unshakable conviction that lemon cheese will fall to pieces on a 250-mile bus trip.

"No such a thing," says Muv. "I know what I'm doing."

And she takes off the closet shelf a big hat box, acquired months earlier at a haberdashery for this specific purpose and well reinforced with heavy cardboard. Into this box, one on top of the other, go the cakes: Pound cake (real butter, ten eggs), lemon cheese and finally that triumph of all Christmas cakes, the Lane cake. (Until I begged her recipe for this book I never was sure what went into a Lane cake except that the layers are put together with a heavenly mixture which includes pecans from Muv's own trees, fresh coconut and something which smells deliciously and suspiciously like brandy.) Between the cakes are acres of tissue paper, paper towels and foil. And the whole thing is then tied together so securely it would be easier to assault Fort Knox than to get past Muv's knots.

From Alford to Atlanta Muv has to fight off the well-intentioned assistance of bus drivers and fellow passengers. In Alford, as in many small towns, everybody knows the bus drivers who pass through twice a day, taking them to the county seat and to do their shopping in neighboring small towns. And these men are solicitous about helping ladies carrying big hat boxes.

Muv will not allow anybody else to touch her box of cakes but if the bus is crowded she will give some young and limber-legged traveler the privilege of standing in the aisle while her cakes ride in state in the seat next to her.

After all, as Miss Minnie, Miss Pearl and Miss Josie say, lemon cheese *is* delicate.

Occasionally in getting ready for Christmas I find that I turn fretful and disgruntled over what I sometimes regard as the Christmas wrapping fetish which has gripped our land. In my day Santa Claus didn't fool around with ribbon and sticky tape and vast expensive sheets of metallic paper. What he couldn't get in the stockings he either hung, naked and unadorned, on the Christmas tree or placed under it.

Of course it was necessary to wrap some few presents for grownups and distant friends and we did this as speedily and unimaginatively as possible, using whatever was left over from last year in the way of paper and ribbon.

We didn't dream a Christmas package was supposed to be an art object. But alas, there comes a time in life when you can't buck the tide. Everybody these days strives for awesomely handsome, unusual and original packages and they think that any really womanly woman is peculiarly endowed by nature to produce same.

But I doubt if my neighbor Jack labors under that delusion now. The other night he came by Sweet Apple bearing a bribe of fireplace logs from his woods and a poke of small gifts which, he engagingly suggested, he was powerless to wrap. Would I be so kind?

Instead of making my anti-wrapping, all-thumbs speech I looked at the oak and hickory, which he was unloading at my door, and I wavered. I took another look and saw six light'ard knots hit the woodpile, like frosting on the cake, and I said I'd be delighted to wrap his presents.

They didn't look so bad when I finished—not when you

consider that some of the paper saved from last year's packages sort of fried when I tried to press it with a hot iron. The grocery bags looked neat enough when I finished trimming them up and tying them on for mail wraps.

It wasn't until the next day when I got to thinking about the project that I realized something was wrong. One of the packages contained lures for a pair of his fishing buddies and one held six antique coin silver spoons for his favorite girl cousin. Had I mixed up the addresses?

The last time I saw my neighbor he was chasing the rural carrier trying to get his packages back. I wonder if fishermen can use that kind of spoon?

It's funny how it takes one little thing to get you in the Christmas mood. You might putter along at plans and preparations for weeks without feeling really Christmasy and then one day suddenly there's some kind of chemical change in the way the day looks, the way you feel. Something inside goes "Zing!" or maybe it's a light and fluttery "Pfff!" and you feel a great rush of joy and excitement.

When my children were little we called it "the Christmas moment" and we noticed year after year that it always came at the same time.

After the school play was over and the commotion of fashioning shepherd clothes out of old draperies and angel wings out of cheesecloth was past, after the name-drawing and the letters to Santa Claus, after the endless Saturdays spent in dime stores and the choir rehearsals and the stocking stuffings at the church . . . after all this there would be one day, maybe grayer and tireder than some, when we would haul out the Christmas angel for the top of the tree. Her wings were made of paper and always sort of frazzled. Her halo was that horrid spun glass stuff that sticks your fingers. One time, back when Mary was teething, one of her feet disappeared.

But every year we took her out with special ceremony and a rush of affection. She had seen us through so much—good years and bad years. She wasn't very decorative but she was ours, and for some reason, Christmas.

The children are out of the nest now and the troubles and griefs that beset us when they were little have grown up along with them. Now when we have a problem it somehow seems to be a bigger problem. Christmas is more complicated than little red rockers and teddy bears under the tree. There are separations and grown-up heartaches—things that can't be solved by just having something to stuff those gaping red stockings.

But the day you find yourself falling prey to that terrible heresy—thinking sad thoughts about Christmas—is the day to take out the Christmas angel.

I was by myself when I hauled the box of tree things from under the stairs the other night. The rain was falling in a slow, lonesome, uncertain way, and fog had drifted up from the hollow and obliterated the woodpile. There was a pile of stuff I wondered why I'd saved, half-melted candy canes and burned-down candles and broken ornaments.

And then I pulled out the angel, slightly refurbished last year and then dealt a telling blow by one of the babies. She was no lovelier than she had been but I held her in my hand and suddenly it was there . . . the Christmas moment.

I turned up the radio and a choir was singing "Silent Night." I poked up the fire and turned on the burner under the soup pot. A great surge of energy gripped me. So much to be done . . . my goodness! Christmas doesn't solve all problems, but without it, many of them—indeed sometimes life itself—would not be bearable.

Since our family has burgeoned so we have decided to be sensible about exchanging gifts. Everything will be for the children, we say, and all the grownups draw names at Thanksgiving so each person has but one thing to buy for another adult.

It's a fine, practical, sensible system, we all assure one another, and the first one not to adhere to it is a rotten egg.

Of course I can't adhere to it absolutely because they're all my children and Muv's my mother and I want to give each of them some little something. Susan is very firm about it, saying often that we shouldn't draw names if we don't stick to it and since she drew Jack's name and bought him some cocktail glasses all her shopping is done—except for a few little things she is assembling to give everybody something to open. Mary agrees that it certainly takes a load off her mind not to have to worry about gifts all around but she works in a bookstore and keeps seeing books that each of us simply must have and she sends them, acting as if it is pure accident that they come at Christmastime.

Muv is probably the worst. She spends months before Christmas making dresses and little pants and rag dolls for the babies and then—just for fun, to have something to unwrap, etc.—she stitches up aprons for the big girls or ruffled pillow shams to go with the handmade quilts she gave them all. Then she comes to town and we all know ahead of time that there will be at least two days of unrelenting shopping for Muv.

She *says* she simply wants to get maybe a nice pair of socks for each of the boys—"something to unwrap" again—and then she comes marching in at bedtime, when the last store has closed, with brimming shopping bags to stuff under the bed and all kinds of whispered conferences with the children over what to do with "you-know-what" in the trunk of one of their cars.

There's no deterring Muv from these rigorous shopping trips. I sometimes beg off from accompanying her by pleading work or illness. But illness doesn't work too well because Muv is bored by infirmities of the flesh.

The other day I told her I thought I had an allergy of some kind. She was busy dressing for town and she said not to fool around with allergies, they were a big nuisance. An old man who lived on the highway near Alford thought he was allergic to traffic and paid six hundred dollars to have his house moved onto a quiet lane at the edge of town. There he found his view was cut off by the corn his neighbors planted and he promptly became allergic to corn and paid six hundred dollars to have his house moved back to the highway.

A bit later I mentioned to Muv that I had a splinter under my fingernail. Such a malady, although small, was a clear indication that I was hard-working and it did hurt—most cruelly, I murmured.

"Have you got a beef gall?" asked Muv, trying to decide if the hat she'd brought to wear to town would go with the suit she was forced by bad weather to put on.

I said I didn't have a smidgen of beef gall.

"Too bad," said Muv. "It would draw the poison right out."

A couple of times I tried to get Muv's attention with a little conjecture as to how I got that splinter under my fingernail but she was quick to divert my thinking from my own paltry woes.

My great-grandmother, she told me, lived in the country and raised twelve children with never an ache nor a pain that she couldn't take care of herself. Once she had a bone felon and she didn't take on the way I was taking on about that little bitty splinter.

"What did she do, Muv?" I asked resignedly.

"Let me out when you stop for the next traffic light," directed Muv, fumbling for her shopping list. "Oh, she stuck her finger in a frog's mouth and tied it shut. Gave her immediate relief."

She slammed the car door and added her last word of direction. "Get a live frog."

For weeks before Christmas I read all the house magazines and think I'm going to do something wondrous in the way of decorating the cabin. I even trek down the road to Maude Miles' and admire all the beautiful wreaths and Della Robbia type swags and things she makes every year. But at the last minute I find myself making the same old garland of pine to hang over the mantel and sticking pine, as usual, in the wrought iron chandelier Jack made to hold candles over the dining table.

Since I've been at Sweet Apple I've given up electric lights for the Christmas tree and use the old-fashioned tin holders with real candles, gifts from people in all kinds of faraway places. We usually light the candles on the tree but once—on Christmas Eve—and then for only a couple of choruses of "Silent Night" which the grownups, for safety's sake, sing while standing with buckets of water and sand in their hands.

We open our packages on Christmas Eve now, too, so that the children can be in their own homes or with other parents on Christmas Day. Because there's always turkey somewhere the next day I try to think of something different to have for dinner on Christmas Eve. It's easy if our friends and Jack's parents, Julia and Lee Morris, come up from the coast for the holiday. They bring quantities of oysters and shrimp and fresh fish and Julia falls to and helps me cook them. But whatever the main course is we always end up with the same dessert we've had as long as I can remember, ambrosia from the cut-glass bowl which was one of Muv's wedding presents, and a choice of three or four different kinds of cake. Once, trying to avoid the tedious task of separating the oranges from their white membranes, I sneaked in a couple of jars of pre-mixed ambrosia from the grocery store but Muv knew the difference immediately and publicized it. Fortunately it tasted all right to me because I had to eat it all myself after Christmas.

When the last sleepy child has been bundled up and loaded into a car for a trip back to town we sometimes linger by the fire, watching the candles gutter in the breeze which blows through the cracks between the logs and the fire on the hearth burn low. Sometimes we reread Christmas cards then and talk of absent friends. I'm always glad to reread the one Vivian Reeves and her daughters send occasionally. It is a poem which Viv's husband, Ollie Reeves, late poet laureate of Georgia, wrote a few years before his death.

The last verse makes the whole reason for the tumultuous preparations, the tiredness and the joy come clear:

Though the stable and the manger and the inn fall into decay
He who walked the world a stranger dwells within our hearts
    today.
Never ending is the story, though the centuries have flown,
First the stable, then the glory of the kingdom and the throne.
Voices of the children blending, Christmas music sweet and gay
And the joy that is unending—Christ the Lord is born today.

Favorite recipes from Sweet Apple

In setting down recipes which are favorites at Sweet Apple I in no way suggest that I am a particularly adept or knowledgeable hand in the kitchen. Practically everybody I know is a better cook than I am. But most of my friends and relations, like cooks everywhere, have their specialties, and if I have any advantage at all it's that each of them has been generous about sharing her specialty with me. Sometimes by faithful application and good luck I can duplicate Olivia's green tomato relish recipe or Verda's corned beef and cabbage and then fall flat on my face trying Julia's baked snapper or one of Muv's cakes.

Frances Tabor, who lives in the little mountain town of Ellijay up the road a piece, is one of the best cooks I know and completely freehanded with her recipes. And no matter how I try I can't make any dish I borrow from her taste as good in my kitchen as it does in hers. I can but conclude that the time, the place and the company—indisputable seasoners of all good cooking—are responsible.

Whatever you eat in that sunny kitchen, overlooking one of the prettiest vegetable gardens in the world, with Herbert

Tabor at one end of the table telling his stories of old days in the mountains, is magnificently seasoned. The tall frame white house where Tabors have lived for many years has a tradition of good food and hospitality going back to pioneer days in the mountains.

Frances, city bred and young when she married, took to mountain cookery as if to the wood range born. She learned from her mother-in-law the art of turning green beans into the succulent, wintertime standby, leather britches. And although canned and frozen green beans are now plentiful in the mountains and in Frances' own kitchen, for that matter, they do not replace leather britches. If you have eaten leather britches on a snowy winter day in the mountains, nothing really replaces them.

So every summer part of the bounteous bean crop in Herbert Tabor's garden goes to make a few bags of leather britches for their own use and to distribute to expatriate mountain friends in all parts of the world, who grow wistful when they think of leather britches.

Beans are selected at their emerald prime, snapped and strung and spread in the sun to dry. Many people use an old window screen and cover the beans with cheesecloth to protect them from bugs. The Tabors have two specially made frames of screen, one to hold the beans, the other to cover them.

For four to five days the beans bask in the sun. They are covered with plastic to protect them from the dew at night or brought in if rain threatens. And then for three or four more days they are dried in the shade. (Frances has a big upstairs storeroom for this.) Finally when the snaps look shriveled and brown and like nothing you'd dream of eating they are ready to store for the winter. Frances learned early that they are prey to weevils and having the city girl's distaste for the small pest that many country people treat casually as something to be scooped from their plate or ignored, she figured out a way to beat them. She spreads the beans on cookie sheets and heats them through in a 200-degree oven. Then she ties them in plastic bags and they are ready to store until that raw, cold winter day when the body and the spirit benefit most from something hot, substantial and tasting of summertime. To cook:

LEATHER BRITCHES

Wash and soak overnight in warm water. Simmer until tender with streak o'lean or ham hock and a pod of red pepper.

Jettie Bell has an equally old-fashioned recipe for preserving summer's beans for winter use, handed down in an old book which her mother kept handy to guide her in everything from culinary enterprises to combating chilblains. The jacket of the book has been missing as long as Jettie Bell can remember, the pages are brittle and yellow and generations of children have done their arithmetic or drawn pictures on its margins. But the bean recipe is clear and useful. It reads:

"Green string beans must be picked when young; put a layer three inches deep in a small wooden keg or half barrel, sprinkle with salt an inch deep, then put another layer of beans, then salt, and beans and salt in alternate layers until you have enough. Let the last be salt. Cover them with a piece of board which will fit the inside of the barrel or keg and place a heavy weight upon it. They will make a brine.

When wanted for use, soak them one night or more in plenty of water, changing it once or twice, until the salt is out of them, then cut them, and boil the same as when fresh."

These briny beans, seldom put up any more since the advent of freezing and the almost continuous supply of fresh beans in the market, are still good. They are, in fact, the forerunner for crisp, zippy beans and "dilly" beans so in vogue today for relishes and salads.

One of my favorites in this department is garlic beans, which you can make from canned or leftover green beans. (If you get canned ones, the Frenched ones look a little prettier.)

GARLIC BEANS

About 4 cups beans
½ cup vinegar
⅓ cup sugar
¾ cup cooking oil
5 fat cloves garlic

Drain beans and immerse in a bath of vinegar, sugar, oil and garlic, which has been run through the garlic press. (I couldn't keep house without this little gadget.) Cover and refrigerate overnight. Drain and serve cold.

Beans grow profligately at Sweet Apple, even outdistancing weeds, which is no small feat. The tender white half-runners may be the best of all, although it's hard to beat the big flat, knotty-looking but surprisingly tender pole bean. We eat them many times a week and I never grow weary of them cooked quickly in as little water as possible and seasoned with a tablespoon or two of bacon drippings with perhaps a slice or two of bacon fried crisp and crumbled over them.

In the days before we moved into the cabin we had a bean patch down by the creek bank on Jack's land and I often cooked beans in my Dutch oven over a few coals by our picnic fire. Ten minutes from garden to pot, unbelievably tender and subtly seasoned by woodsmoke, those beans were probably the best beans I ever cooked. I still strive to match them and the nearest I come is when there's not a drop of water to spare in the pot when the beans are done and the cooking has taken no more than twenty minutes.

(This is a cross between the unnaturally bright green beans flavored with a bit of butter, which is the new fashion in the city and among dieters, and the old-time, country style method of cooking beans long and slowly and serving them swimming in liquor with great chunks of fatback or ham.)

New potatoes have a natural affinity for green beans and in the summer it seems a sacrilege, even if you're dieting, not to cook a few small potatoes, gently scrubbed and scraped, in the pot with the beans.

A variation on the bean theme is to bathe string beans in a vinaigrette sauce, the juice of a lemon, a tablespoonful chopped parsley and two or three small sweet pickles or gherkins chopped fine.

There have been times when I am in a casserole phase

(this hits me every year or so when I cast about for a prepare-ahead dish or am having females to lunch) that I have immersed beans in mushroom soup, grated cheese and slivered almonds. Such a dish, topped with bread crumbs or crushed cornflakes and browned in the oven, turns out fine—about like anything else you want to cook in the same mixture. Hardly *beany* and certainly not something to put before a man, unless you happen to have a rare one who is not suspicious of casseroles in general and anything blanketed in mushroom soup in particular.

Another kind of beans which strengthens and sustains us at Sweet Apple is the dried red kidney bean. This is not indigenous to north Georgia, I'm afraid, where all dried beans are unjustly associated with lean fare or wash day. It is particularly beloved in New Orleans, where no restaurant is too elegant to feature red beans and rice at least once a week. Most of them, particularly the plain ones patronized by working people, offer red beans and rice every day.

One Saturday after hours of roaming around the French Quarter a friend and I were exhausted and hungry and had our minds set on dropping by that wonderful old delicatessen, Solari's, and lunching on red beans and rice. To our disappointment, they weren't on the menu that day. We were about to order something else when a gentleman two seats down the counter interrupted with the easy New Orleans familiarity and hospitality.

"You want red beans?" he asked. "You get 'em to da Roosevelt *Saturdays*."

The waitress understood our need and graciously waved us off to the Roosevelt Hotel dining room.

There are many ways of serving red beans and rice but we

are partial to Jack Strong's recipe at Sweet Apple. Reared on the Mississippi coast and in New Orleans, he abhors the makeshift inland way of using canned beans and has shopped around until he knows the more reliable sources of packaged dried beans. Not surprisingly these are usually stores in the poorer sections of town where a pound package of beans for thirteen cents is still an important bargain.

JACK'S RED BEANS

    1 1-pound package dried red kidney beans
    3 medium Bermuda onions (others will do)
    3 cloves garlic
    3 medium ham hocks (lean)
    2 teaspoons salt
    1 tablespoon oleo or salad oil for sautéeing

Wash and put beans on to boil in a large heavy bottom pot of iron or aluminum with a cover. (A four-quart pot will be a bit crowded but will suffice.) Dice onions and sauté until they are transparent. Mince garlic and sauté separately from the onions— this to make sure the garlic gets sautéed. Scrape onions and garlic directly into the water and beans. Place the ham hocks in the pot with the beans and add the salt after the water has started boiling. (Salt keeps the beans whole. If it is not added early beans may cook to pieces.) Use lean ham hocks whole but trim most of the fat from fatty ham hocks. After the beans have begun to boil turn down heat and simmer for about 4 hours or longer until beans are tender. Additional water may be required as ingredients cook down.

Some cooks stir the beans and have a reddish gravy with them. Jack prefers no stirring and liquid that remains clear.

RICE

The accompaniment for red beans is, of course, rice. It is not a north Georgia specialty either but a staple of my childhood. We ate it at least once a day in south Alabama—always as a vegetable at dinner, which was our mid-day meal then—sometimes with cold milk for supper and now and then in pudding. One of the first tasks I learned to perform in the kitchen as a child was that daily rite: "Put on the rice."

This was done by washing a cupful of rice in cold water until it ran clear and then putting it on to boil in a cupful of water with a teaspoonful of salt. When it comes to a brisk boil, turn the heat low, cover and let simmer for about 20 minutes or until dry and fluffy.

A more foolproof method, I have found in recent years, is to put the rice on in a quart or more of rapidly boiling salted water and cook until the grains are soft but not mushy. Drain, rinse in a colander with cold water and set back over a pot of boiling water to steam. (If you let this process go on too long—hours, that is—the top grains of rice will dry out and harden, which gives my method a bad name among Gulf Coast friends. Otherwise, it strikes me that the rice is lighter and dryer and there's the additional advantage of not having a lot of it stick to the pot.)

Either way you cook your rice you will want a plateful of it when you ladle on red beans with their rich juice and the chunks of lean ham. Some people enjoy further spicing their plates with a lacing of Louisiana red hot or Louisiana green hot, that condiment of liquid fire which can be purchased at most grocery stores.

The meal can be more sophisticated with a tossed green salad, a loaf of crusty French bread and a bottle of French table wine.

I have heard of people using leftover beans in salad but I can never bring myself to tamper with perfection. Cold red beans eaten with a spoon out of a refrigerator dish at midnight set well with me and one of my favorite mid-morning snacks, after fishing on the gulf from before dawn, was a sandwich made of Julia's leftover beans and French bread. Other members of the party contended that the ham from the beans and hot mustard made an even better sandwich but I never could relinquish my hold on beans long enough to try.

To show you in what esteem the dried bean is held in New Orleans, the *Picayune Original Creole Cook Book* earnestly points out that "In the colleges and convents where large numbers of children are sent to be reared to be strong and useful men and women, several times a week there appears on the table the nicely cooked dish of Red Beans, which are eaten with rice. . . . The Creoles hold that the boys and girls who are raised on beans and rice and beef will be among the strongest and sturdiest of people."

It is certainly one of the ways we keep up our strength at Sweet Apple.

One of the things that endears rice to me is its talent for being as plain or as festive as you choose. It's cheap, filling and easy to keep on hand. I consider my provisions are running dangerously low when the old blue half-gallon fruit jar on the cupboard shelf isn't at least half full of long-grained white rice. A package of brown rice is a pleasant change and my idea of real opulence is to have in reserve a package of the prohibitively expensive wild rice.

Jack's version of "dirty" rice, another Creole favorite, stuffs or goes with broiled or baked chicken, Cornish hen or quail. I like it because the complicated additions can be prepared a day ahead, wrapped in foil and refrigerated until just before the meal when you have your rice, either white or brown, fluffy and hot.

DIRTY RICE A LA STRONG

2 large or 3 medium Bermuda onions, chopped
1 pound cooked ham, diced
½ pound pecans, halves or pieces
1 teaspoon salt
1 teaspoon black pepper
½ teaspoon cayenne, if you like the heat
2 tablespoons oleo or butter

Sauté onions in 1 tablespoon of oleo or butter until they are transparent, not brown; add seasonings. Frizzle the ham 5 or 6 minutes. Lightly parch the pecans in oleo or butter. Mix with hot dry rice and heat through, reserving pecans for last because they have a tendency to lose their crispness if kept waiting too long.

This is good as a stuffing but better, to my notion,

if heaped on a large platter and surrounded with birds. Some people like the giblets boiled until tender in salted water, chopped and added to the rice. I'm not partial to giblets either for their individual flavor or the way they muddy the color of the rice but them as likes them may use them.

A slightly simpler and quicker rice for chicken or other birds is:

SAVANNAH RICE

1 cup cooked rice
½ stick butter or oleo
1 tablespoon chopped parsley

Melt butter or oleo in a heavy pot, add rice, sprinkle with parsley. (Dried parsley flakes will do if you haven't the fresh.)

And one of my very favorite versions of rice calls for a cup of pecans, chopped fine and untoasted, half a cup of chopped young onions added to the cooked rice.

OKRA

An unending surprise to me in cooking is that you never know when you are plagiarizing. Just as two or three great minds hit upon major discoveries in science and invention almost simultaneously, so several people may discover the same new way of cooking an old staple at the same time. Okra grows well in southern gardens and is standard summertime fare on southern tables.

In fact it is so essential to soups and seafood gumbos that our late friend, Frank Gutierrez, used to tell of an old neighbor of French extraction whose standard greeting was: "How's yo' okras, Frank?"

Not how are you, how is your wife or your business but how is that minimum requisite to life and well-being, your okra patch.

The first garden we had at Sweet Apple was a prodigious producer of okra and in order to keep up with it we devised many ways of eating okra. A favorite way is to gather the pods with a bit of stem attached while they are in mere infancy—three inches long at most, preferably less—and then run with them to the kitchen where a pot of salted water is already boiling, plunk them into the pot and check the time. Meanwhile, in an ovenproof ramekin have half a stick of butter melting, to which add the juice of half a lemon. When the okra has boiled 5 to 7 minutes, depending on its size, lift it out with a slotted spoon to avoid piercing its tender young skin, of course, and arrange in a circle around a dish of butter and lemon juice. The nubbin of stem left on the end makes a handy holder for the people on the terrace who will dip the okra in the butter and lemon juice and eat it as an appetizer.

We had been eating this delicacy a full summer before we discovered almost the exact recipe in Marjorie Kinnan Rawlings' *Cross Creek Cookery*. I believe she served hers as an appetizer, too, but had the additional information that you best allow 12 pods of okra per person—a detail I had to learn by experience.

The tendency of okra to sliminess kept me from valuing it as I should for years. This failing is avoided in the foregoing recipe by keeping the okra skin unbroken and not overcooking it. I find that the addition of lemon juice to the water in which okra is boiling also helps.

A few pods of young okra are a great addition to a pot of field peas and butter beans in the summertime. They should be added 10 or 15 minutes before the peas are ready to serve —not longer or they'll cook to pieces.

Other uses of okra which we have enjoyed:

FRIED OKRA

Wash the pods and slice in rounds, salt, lightly dip in corn meal and fry in just enough fat to keep from sticking. Brown lightly, turning often to keep from burning. Drain on paper towels. If you happen to like a less crisp okra you may add a few tablespoons of water and finish the cooking with the okra covered.

FRENCH FRIED OKRA

Select young pods leaving stem end on, wash, dry on paper towel, salt and dip in beaten egg and milk, then flour and fry in deep fat. Drain on paper towel but only briefly. They should be eaten while they're hot and crisp.

OKRA CREOLE

4 dozen pods okra
1 can tomatoes or three fresh ones
1 green bell pepper
1 medium onion
Garlic, salt, pepper, chopped parsley

Wash okra, cut into rounds, boil in salted water to which a little lemon juice has been added, for about 6 or 7 minutes. Meanwhile, sauté chopped onion, minced garlic and chopped green pepper in about a tablespoonful of bacon drippings. Add tomatoes and okra. Simmer for about 20 minutes, seasoning with salt and pepper—a dash of cayenne, if you want to be authentic—and garnish with parsley.

There's no overestimating the importance of okra to soup and particularly seafood gumbo. Small whole pods of okra also make wonderful pickles but the trick, making them crisp, is one I've never mastered. So when we feel the need for pickled okra we buy it from the gourmet shelf in the grocery store.

Southerners are inclined to make a good deal over having been "raised po'ah." I suppose joking about it, which invites the participation of even the more affluent, made the reality of scant rations less harsh. In the country particularly you hear frequent references to hard times. There is even a road near Sweet Apple which memorializes tough going. It's called Hardscrabble.

One day up at Chadwick's store some of the old-timers were discussing Depression days and one raconteur sought to overreach them all.

"Shoot, I remember," he said, "when things was so tight you prayed every fall the persimmons would hold out till the poke sallet come up in the spring."

Things probably weren't literally that bad with many people but the most graphic lesson I ever had about the rigors of Reconstruction days following the Civil War was given to me by my Great Aunt Dilly, who was a teen-ager in 1865. I remember as a child seeing her eat cold corn bread and cold collard greens for breakfast when I was delicately toying with my orange juice. Caught between distaste and awe I asked her how she could stand such fare so early in the morning.

"I say, how can I 'stand it'!" she repeated, cruelly mimicking my finicky tone. "If you had been raised when I was you'd be mighty glad to get any kind of food. You et it when you got it—lest somebody else beat you to it!"

Except for the timing, Aunt Dilly's dish of collards and corn bread, like so many items of plain country fare, had a great deal to commend it to the attention of gourmets. I don't recommend cold collards and corn bread and I especially don't recommend them for breakfast but there are certain seasons of the year when nothing tastes so good as collards which have been touched by frost, gathered while they are still young and crisp and cooked with smoked bacon.

Naturally they must have hot corn bread to go with them —to my taste a plain hoecake of corn bread cooked in an iron skillet on top of the stove with only water, salt and bacon drippings to season it. There are many kinds of corn bread and they all have their place. The place of plain skillet corn bread is, I submit, at the side of collards or, at the very least, mustard or turnip greens. Corn muffins, egg bread, crackling bread or the little crisp corncakes may be happily wed to any vegetable dinner.

COLLARD GREENS

Select the tenderest leaves and wash them well, nipping off the tough stems. Cut the leaves crosswise into ribbons about an inch wide. (I use kitchen shears for this.) Put on in just enough cold water to cover with a chunk of smoked bacon scored deeply or a lean ham hock. (A three-inch square of bacon is about right for the usual market bunch of greens.) Boil slowly an hour or longer until the greens are tender and most of the water is cooked away. A bottle of hot pepper sauce is a must in the household where greens are a staple. Each diner dribbles it on his greens at his own discretion—or risk.

TURNIP GREENS

Turnip greens are available in Georgia almost year-round. They are among the first things up in the garden in the spring, along with lettuce and English peas, and they reappear again in the fall, surviving light frosts sometimes almost until Christmas. A really killing freeze, however, will get them. After they are no longer available in local gardens we stop by the Municipal Market in Atlanta and buy greens that have been trucked up from south Georgia or Florida.

Being a working woman I make full use of my pressure cooker and never more happily than with turnip greens. For one thing, the picking and washing of turnip greens is such a time-consuming task I'd be in the kitchen all night if I didn't have something to speed up the cooking. I learned from Muv to take one leaf at the time, inspect it carefully for bugs or wilted spots and break off its stem. (Some cooks use the stems but Muv contends they are bitter and stringy.) Every leaf must be lovingly washed, starting with tepid water and working up to cold water. I once heard of a woman who washed her greens in her washing machine but I haven't had the nerve to try that.

While the green picking and washing process is going on I give a chunk of smoked bacon or two or three slices of breakfast bacon and the turnip roots, peeled and sliced, a three-minute headstart in the pressure cooker, using as little water as possible. The greens are added, relying mostly on the water that sticks to them to keep them afloat. It is seldom necessary to add water to turnip greens and the less the better.

Five minutes is enough time in the pressure cooker, perhaps twenty or at the most thirty in an ordinary pot or your Dutch oven. (Overboiling greens makes them dark and slick and tasteless.) When you have sampled a leaf and find it tender and done, drain the liquor off and reserve for dunking with corn bread at some time when your spirits and energy are low. Chop the greens fine, using two knives, and adjust the seasoning. Sometimes it is necessary to add salt—if your bacon wasn't salty enough—and a tablespoon or two of bacon drippings.

MUSTARD GREENS

The curly, bright-green mustard is a delight of the early spring when winter-tired palates crave something fresh and different. We often put small mustard leaves in green salads, where they look pretty and add a piquant, slightly hot taste.

Many people boil mustard as they do turnip greens and collards but at Sweet Apple we are wilted mustard fans. Fry two or three pieces of breakfast bacon crisp and remove from skillet, sauté a few young green onions (chopped) in the fat and remove. Cram in (this takes a bit of doing) the washed and picked mustard with only the water that clings to the leaves. The hot fat will wilt it fairly fast so you can get a sizable bunch of mustard into a big skillet or, again, your Dutch oven. Cover and cook only until thoroughly wilted and tender. Drain, chop and serve with bits of bacon and onions distributed evenly through the greens.

SPINACH

One summer I had a love affair with Malabar spinach, the climbing kind, and although we haven't grown it since, we bring spinach of some kind home from the market almost once a week. Malabar spinach makes a fine decorative vine, which covered the back fence for me but really took off in the Tabors' garden, festooning a trellis with rich swags of green, clambering up the walls of their house and shading the upstairs porch. They cropped leaves daily, distributed them widely to all their neighbors and froze quantities of them.

Frances' way of cooking it serves equally well for any spinach. Wash, as for turnip greens, except that Malabar, being grandly aloof from the dirt, doesn't need much washing. Steam for ten minutes in the water that clings to the leaves. Add lemon juice, butter, a teaspoonful of sugar, salt, a dollop of cream and eat—fast and joyfully.

POKE SALLET

Pokeweed grows wild around all the roadsides, barn lots and old house sites in Sweet Apple settlement. As it matures its stems turn deep red and it produces a crop of purple berries, which look much like elderberries but are poisonous. According to country lore, poke leaves themselves are poisonous unless you get them very young and parboil them carefully. I read somewhere that this is not strictly true, that the young leaves are safe without parboiling. All I can think is *how* young is young? My authority on woodcraft, Horace Kephart (*Camping and Woodcraft*) clearly says that the mature shoots are poisonous. So far I have not had the courage to cook poke myself but I have enjoyed it tremendously when cooked by Verda.

Her recipe calls for parboiling the washed leaves about ten minutes, pouring off the water and starting over with fresh. She seasons it as for mustard or turnip greens. As a lagniappe Verda saves the poke sallet stems, boils them in salt water, drains and covers them with vinegar. This makes a pleasant relish with any meat dish and I have kept them in the refrigerator for weeks.

Greens without corn bread, as I may have suggested once or twice, are like spring without violets, a fiddle without a bow.

OVEN CORN BREAD

Oven corn bread is foolproof and I bake it almost every day in the summer when we're having a vegetable dinner and always at Thanksgiving or Christmas when a big pan of it is needed for Muv to make her celebrated corn bread dressing.

For an eight-inch square pan of bread I use:

> 1 cup corn meal (preferably water-ground)
> ½ teaspoon salt
> 3 teaspoons baking powder
> 1 egg
> 3 tablespoons cooking oil
> 1 cup milk

Grease the pan and set the oven at 375 degrees before sifting meal, salt and baking powder together. Add cooking oil. Beat egg slightly and add to meal with milk. Bake until brown and springy.

This is meltingly good with Artie Cox's country butter. Sometimes, as at Christmas and Thanksgiving, I have to double the recipe. The important thing is to always use as much milk as you use meal.

The mixture will be soupy but it turns out fine in the end.

SKILLET CORN BREAD

1 cup corn meal
½ teaspoon salt
Enough boiling water to make a rather thick batter that will hold its shape when turned into skillet
Enough bacon drippings or cooking oil to grease the skillet well

Mix salt and corn meal and stir in boiling water. Turn in to hot but not smoking skillet or griddle and cook slowly. You will need to upend your skillet over a plate to turn your hoecake but a couple of spatulas will do if you are using a griddle.

Thin this batter slightly to make little corncakes. Slightly richer, crunchier ones may be made by adding 3 tablespoonfuls of melted butter to the basic meal and salt mixture and cooking on a cookie sheet in a 375-degree oven for about 20 minutes.

CRACKLING BREAD

Country people who still kill their own hogs take crackling bread for granted but city people have to make do with store-bought cracklings which, I know from Muv, must be selected with care. Muv goes down the aisles between the stalls at the Municipal Market, inspecting cracklings with a gimlet eye and she never buys until she has sampled a crackling or two from at least three vendors. Cracklings, of course, are what's left when the fat pork has been "rendered" to make lard. It goes without saying that they will be fat but according to Muv they must not be too fat. A proper crackling, in order to have the requisite nutty flavor, has a smidgen of lean meat on it.

Before the advent of refrigeration crackling bread was strictly a fall and winter delicacy. Now it can be had year 'round, although it is a little rich for summertime eating, to my taste.

To make it: Combine 2 cups of water-ground meal with 1 teaspoon salt and 3 teaspoons baking powder. Stir in 1 cup milk which has either been thinned with water or is skimmed, 1 egg and ¾ cup cracklings. Bake in an iron skillet, which has been lightly greased, in a 400-degree oven for about 30 minutes.

ASH CAKES

When we bake our corn bread on the hearth at Sweet Apple we use foil, wrapping each individual dollop of the skillet corn bread mixture in a separate swatch. In the old days a real corn bread virtuoso merely swept a clean place on the hearth, covered it with hot ashes, lined up the cakes or pone and covered them with more hot ashes. The result was a wonderfully golden brown, deliciously flavored corn-cake that could be brushed clean of ashes. On the coast they used to use fig leaves between the cakes and ashes.

HUSHPUPPIES

There is yet another kind of corn bread that goes strictly with fish—the fabled hushpuppy. This delicacy has fallen into disrepute because of the greasy variety with the gooey center served at so many roadside catfish eateries. But properly cooked, particularly on the banks of the stream where you caught the fish, it has few equals.

Mix together 1 cup corn meal, 2 teaspoons baking powder, ½ teaspoon salt. Add a chopped onion. Beat in 1 egg and enough water to make the meal hold together when you shape it into balls the size of golf balls. Make an indentation in each ball so it will brown well. Cook in deep fat, from which you have just removed your fried fish, and serve immediately. (There's nothing less appetizing than a cold hushpuppy.)

These are all things that are cheap, filling and remarkably satisfying to the southern-born but I am aware that people in other sections of the country may have to learn to like them. And some, of course, never consider it worth the trouble.

As we cherish our corn bread, so do we esteem those other corn products, grits and hominy. Old-fashioned ladies in Mobile and Savannah use the words interchangeably. "A nice dish of hominy" to them may well mean grits, eaten always at breakfast and sometimes with hash for supper.

To my neighbors in north Georgia hominy always refers to the whole-grained corn, which has been soaked in lye water until it loses its husk and then seasoned, simmered with meat and served as a vegetable at dinner. Frances Tabor learned from her mother-in-law the art of making her own lye hominy and when I naively asked if it was better than the canned kind, on which I was reared, Herbert Tabor snorted.

"About as much difference between homemade lye hominy and canned as there is between chicken and 'possum!" he said.

It's true. Homemade lye hominy is far superior to the canned variety—and well it should be because it takes about a full day to make it, if you are fortunate enough to get mature, well-dried, weevil-free corn, which Frances insists upon.

She uses about eight ears of corn, which makes a bountiful supply of hominy, enough to share with the neighbors and to have on hand in the refrigerator for weeks for the steady stream of hungry visitors to the Tabor house. She makes this batch about twice a year.

LYE HOMINY

Shell 8 ears of corn and wash thoroughly, put in an enameled dishpan (enameled only, Frances specifies), cover with warm water in which you have dissolved 1 level teaspoon Red Devil lye. Cover with foil and cook for 2 hours, stirring occasionally. The husks will begin to come off and the water will be red. Drain through a colander, being careful not to get your hands in the water. Let warm water from the tap run over the corn for a few minutes. Cover again with warm water and return to the stove to simmer. Every 2 or 3 hours drain, rinse and change the water. The husks will gradually come off with this treatment. When the corn is white and husk free and the water is clear the hominy is done.

Then, says Herbert Tabor, it is "fit" to season with butter, salt and pepper and eat with a side dish of crisp fried chit'lings (chitterlings). Since Frances won't have the fragrant pig's intestines, even those out of a can and presumably hospital-clean and sterile, cooked in her kitchen while she's there, Mr. Tabor has to make do with fried country ham, red-eye gravy and biscuits.

When Frances goes visiting or to town to shop, her husband sometimes invites in a few cronies and cooks up a batch of chitterlings himself, cutting the creamy lengths into three- or four-inch pieces, dipping them in egg and milk and then into flour and frying them in deep fat until they're crisp and brown. Frances vows she can smell them cooking at the city limits and promptly hurries home and throws up the windows and airs out the kitchen.

Store-bought lye hominy cooked with a bit of ham or bacon and salted and well peppered is a sustaining dish but not inspiring. Back when you could buy a No. 2 can for ten cents I did considerable experimenting with hominy and found that you can give it glamour by mashing it slightly and adding it to scrambled eggs, mixing it with crisp fried bacon and tomato pulp and filling tomato shells with it and baking it or flossing it up with cheese sauce.

CHEESE HOMINY

Cover 2 cups of hominy (either canned or homemade) with a good white sauce to which you have added 1 cup grated cheese, 1/4 teaspoon dried mustard and a dash of cayenne. Bake about 15 minutes in a medium oven. Garnish with parsley or bacon curls and serve.

GRITS

In these days of calory counting we don't have grits every day but when there's company or time for a leisurely breakfast and especially when there's grief or trouble in the family, I find myself turning automatically to grits. There's something comforting about grits—hot and creamy and bland, resting beneficently on the tired and troubled stomach.

A few years ago I embroiled myself in a controversy by referring to grits as "they." Readers chose up sides and bombarded me with letters on the subject. When the tumult and the shouting died down and I had sorted over the letters I came to the conclusion that those who saw grits as a singular noun were perhaps more knowledgeable about grammar. But those who regard grits as plural were the true grits fans.

Among the authorities cited for "they" are Marjorie Kinnan Rawlings, a woman with both a flair for food and some little success with the language, and the *Picayune Original Creole Cook Book* which calls *them* "Du Gru Bouilli" and rhapsodizes: "In any manner in which they are served, they are always palatable."

When I was a child grits cooking was a long and slow process. Sometimes we soaked them overnight. They had to be washed, as Muv always directed me, "until the water runs clear." Nowadays I buy the quick-cooking kind, obey the package order not to wash, and can't tell the difference.

The standard directions are about 1 cup of grits to 4 cups of water and 1 teaspoon of salt. Cook 5 to 7 minutes.

On Sunday mornings I keep the grits hot in a double boiler

and enhance their creamy consistency by stirring in a little butter and, if no dieter is watching, a dash or two of coffee cream.

Once we had a friend from New York who tried valiantly to enjoy our breakfast grits, served, of course, with bacon and scrambled or fried eggs. He never became a bonafide grits fan until one night he discovered cheese grits. Then he was hooked. He simply couldn't have cheese grits too often and I remember coming home from work to find him in my kitchen grating cheese and leading my children in singing—to the tune of the Toreador Song from "Carmen"—an aria he had composed to grits. Half a cup of grated cheese is about right to stir into a potful of grits just before serving.

Nowadays when I have leftover grits I feed them to the birds. Muv used to sauté an onion in a couple of tablespoons of bacon fat, mash up the grits with a fork and heat them through in the skillet with onion and fat and sprinkle liberally with black pepper. This was a hot and doubtless nourishing supper dish but it never really caught on with me.

Some better is the method of slicing cold cooked grits into wedges, dipping in egg and milk and frying until brown in bacon fat or butter. With a dollop of Mrs. Walter Geer's May haw jelly, with which I am endowed occasionally, and a glass of milk this makes a good Sunday night snack.

A rather more fancy breakfast dish is:

BAKED GRITS

Boil 1 cup of grits in 2 cups of water and 2 cups of milk with 1 teaspoon of salt. Cool slightly and turn into a baking dish, mixing in 2 beaten egg yolks. When egg yolks are well blended add 2 egg whites, which have been beaten quite stiff, and ½ cup of cream. Bake in a medium oven for 10 or 15 minutes, until golden brown.

This is also a pleasant Sunday night supper dish if you were planning to have only leftover roast and feel the need of something hot or have unexpected company. It is a cousin to the southern spoon bread of song and story.

Aunt Nancy Pankey, who, as this is written, approaches her ninety-eighth birthday, is a veteran of hard times in the southern mountains. She married a man much older than she was—a Confederate veteran—and was widowed at an early age with a big family of children to feed on the rough and rocky mountain farm left to her.

Many a day, Aunt Nancy told me, she came "weakling in from the field," drank a little water sweetened with sorghum for sustenance and went back to work. At night she wove baskets from honeysuckle vines to sell on the town square in Ellijay to earn money for what they couldn't grow on the farm.

But as her boys grew up and the farm flourished, Mrs. Pankey grew in stature as a cook. Like most mountain cooks her mettle was tested, her virtuosity displayed at such eating events as Decoration Day at the church, at family reunions and at protracted meetings—the summertime revival which is still called "revival-roas'n'ear" meeting. It gets its name, of course, from its timing. Revivals were set to coincide with the ripening of roasting ears in the corn patch and lay-by time on the farm, when the crops were in and flourishing and the farmer could take a breather before the harvest.

A happily timed revival, according to Mr. Tabor, was one that coincided also with the ripening of the watermelons about July 4.

In addition to the meals served on long tables under the trees in the churchyard there was the pressing business of setting a good table in the household honored by the presence of visiting preachers. To have the preachers stay at one's house was a thing of status and cooks always out-did themselves to merit such attention by the bounty and splendor of their cuisine.

As a little boy at the turn of the century Mr. Tabor remembers well the commotion the approach of preachers set off in kitchen, pantry, smokehouse and springhouse and the final triumph of Sunday dinner with three or four kinds of meat, chicken, every vegetable known to the farm, cucumbers, tomatoes, pickles, jams, jellies, relishes, two or three kinds of bread, sourwood honey, cookies, cakes, pies and strawberries and cream.

His task as a little boy was to keep the fly fan in motion over the long dining-room table while the grownups did justice to the meal. This was, for a child, an agonizingly deliberate ritual which called for eating, talking, rearing back to loosen belts and more eating and more talking. Watching and waiting, the little boy grew faint with hunger and developed a distaste for Methodist preachers which he was years overcoming.

The signal that the meal was over was sounded when his father, loosening his belt another notch, stood up, sighed and paid his wife this fulsome compliment:

"Well, Kate, what little there was of it done tolerable well."

My neighbors still cook prodigiously for Decoration Day and Homecoming Day at the church—that Sunday in the spring when everybody comes back to Ebenezer or New Home or Old Shiloh or Bethany to hear day-long preaching and singing, to decorate the graves of the departed in the little churchyard and to feast from long tables set up under the trees.

At these meetings dinner is "spread together," which is to say every dish is set forth for general enjoyment. But old hands always recognize the viands of the premier cooks in the community and make a beeline for what they know is going to be of unparalleled excellence in its field.

From an old notebook I kept I find a list I jotted down at one such fete. I was bug-eyed then and I still am at the variety and the quantity. Under heading of meats alone there was fried chicken, baked chicken, broiled chicken and chicken pie. There was ham, whole and magnificently dressed in a brown sugar glaze and wreathed with sweet potatoes and tart little apples quartered and cooked in butter and brown sugar. There was also fried ham, roast beef, roast lamb, meat loaf, sausage, baked pork chops and squirrel pie. (Not too many years ago, Mr. Tabor told me, there would also have been venison, bear and possibly rabbit.)

Most of these dishes are standard fare, to be found in all parts of the country, with the possible exception of the squirrel pie. Lest any reader find herself with squirrel on hand and no counsel forthcoming from her standard cookbooks on its preparation, I happen to have a splendid recipe from the University of Georgia, College of Agriculture, "Cooking Wild Game" bulletin.

Squirrel, says this authority, does not have the "gamey" taste present in most wild animals, so soaking is unnecessary and parboiling advisable only for "the oldest and toughest animals." To make:

SQUIRREL PIE

Disjoint and cut squirrel into 2 or 3 pieces. Cover with water and cook 1 hour. Remove meat from bones in large pieces. Add 3 tablespoons flour, 1 teaspoon salt, ⅛ teaspoon pepper and ½ cup cut mushrooms to the stock, which should measure about 2 cups. If less, add milk. Pour into a baking dish and top with biscuit crust and bake 30 to 40 minutes at 350 degrees.

For biscuit crust sift 2 cups flour, 4 teaspoons baking powder and ½ teaspoon salt. Cut in ¼ cup shortening and stir in ⅔ cup milk. Roll only enough to make it fit the baking dish.

(To show you how sensitive these game experts are at the University, their recipes for muskrat meat loaf, baked stuffed muskrat and fried muskrat are preceded with this note: "We use the real name for the animal involved here but you might want to substitute the expression 'marsh rabbit' before you put these recipes in your file. People are funny.")

We may be in a rut at Sweet Apple but we haven't tried muskrat under either name yet. We noticed that the 'possum population was burgeoning and discussed the idea of trapping and cooking one. At that time our neighbor, Clarence Johnson, was trapping them for Emory University Medical School's research department and getting five dollars a head for all he could find, big or little. We concluded that ham, chicken or steak—hackneyed old standbys—might be cheaper per pound, especially after we had a report from Mr. Lum Crow on the subject.

Mr. Crow said he liked 'possum fine and had some little experience in cooking it, roasting it in the oven until the fat bubbled and crisped up and serving it with baked sweet potatoes.

"When did you have 'possum last, Mr. Crow?" I asked.

"About sixty year ago," he said. "Before I married Dessie."

TURTLE

Turtles found Jack's lake and moved in in such numbers Jack was worried about the small fish population. Quinton Johnson, who keeps his freezer stocked with rabbits and squirrels, said he would like to have a few turtles on hand. He set a big wire trap in Jack's lake, baiting it with some raw chicken, and in no time at all the turtles were transferred from Jack's lake to Quinton's kitchen.

After you have cleaned a turtle, which is a task roughly approximating cleaning a Brink's armored truck, wash the meat in salt water or water with a little vinegar in it. If it is a young turtle you can dip it in flour and fry it, as chicken. Old turtles make delicious soup or stew and are surprisingly unfishy tasting, Quinton tells me.

CHICKEN

Chickens, being one of Georgia's principal crops, are plentiful in the market, usually cheap, both money-wise and calory-wise, and we have them often at Sweet Apple. When the price goes down to twenty-two to twenty-five cents a pound I buy three or four and put them in the freezer against the weekend when the children arrive unexpectedly and I haven't planned anything special.

Fried chicken, a fabled Old South specialty, can be perfectly dreadful—greasy on the outside and underdone near the bone. To avoid these errors takes time and loving care and it bores me stiff to stand in the house and fry chicken when everybody else is doing something more interesting outside. For that reason, more often than not, we have some version of oven-cooked chicken.

ROAST CHICKEN

For some reason fryers come cheaper whole than cut up and I frequently roast them instead of buying the usual hen for roasting. Lemon juice is a good seasoner for many things and particularly for chicken, I think.

So I divest young chickens of their giblets and neck, which usually come wrapped in paper and tucked in the body cavity, wipe clean with a damp paper towel, salt and pepper inside and out. Peel a small onion and stick in the cavity whole, along with a lump or two of butter. Rub outside of chicken with butter and put in a baking dish with enough water to keep it from sticking until the juices start flowing. Bake in a 375-degree oven, basting occasionally with lemon juice, until drumsticks waggle easily, telling you it's done.

FRYER WITH LEMON

For a cut-up fryer you can vary the recipe somewhat, rubbing lemon juice on each piece of chicken and then rolling lightly in a mixture of flour, salt and paprika. Here, as elsewhere when cooking chicken or anything that needs flouring, it is simpler and easier to put flour and salt and pepper in a paper bag and shake a few chicken pieces at the time in the mixture. Brown chicken quickly in about 4 tablespoons of cooking oil and then arrange in a baking dish. Sprinkle a few grains of brown sugar over the chicken, cover with thin lemon slices, pour in 1 cup of chicken broth and bake about 40 minutes at 375 degrees. A cup of red wine will serve instead of the broth, if you happen to like it. In fact, you may brown the chicken early in the morning and marinate it in the wine until just before dinnertime.

CHICKEN AND DUMPLINGS

This is a dish we have only when Muv comes because I am intimidated by the chances of failure with dumplings. The business of not lifting the lid for the duration of the cooking worries me and there are weather signs that bode ill for dumplings.

Frances Tabor says her mother-in-law, Miss Kate, refused to make dumplings on any but the fairest of days. When her family urged her she would say, "Can't you see it's cloudy? They'd taste like feathers today!"

I've always been afraid my dumplings would taste the opposite—like lead. But Muv makes a superior pot of chicken and dumplings at the drop of a hat. In the mountains she cooked a tough old hen with an onion and a couple of stalks of celery in a covered iron pot on the fireplace most of one day and when we all got in from a hike in the afternoon she quickly rolled and cut her dumplings, dropped them in the simmering pot, covered them and by some instinct lifted the lid at the precise second they were ready.

Most cooks say it takes dumplings 12 minutes but I think that is because they drop their dumpling batter into the pot by the spoonful, making thick dumplings. Muv's dumplings are thin and, since she doesn't pay any attention to the clock, I borrowed—for its timing—the recipe of her good friend Miss Minnie (Mrs. L. F.) Syfrett from the little collection of recipes the Woman's Society of Christian Service of the Alford Methodist Church put out to raise money for missionaries.

MISS MINNIE'S DUMPLINGS

2 tablespoons buttermilk
¾ cup water
2 cups self-rising flour

Mix milk, water and self-rising flour, use additional flour to roll dough thin. Cut in small squares

and drop into boiling chicken. Let simmer 10 minutes, cover and remove from heat.

If you don't use self-rising flour—and I don't—
I think 1 teaspoon of baking powder and ½ teaspoon salt will be needed when you sift.

FRIED CHICKEN

If there comes a time when you have your heart set on
fried chicken and are willing to stay in the kitchen with it,
cooking it slowly and tenderly, I heartily recommend the
method used by Marianne Lambert's cook, Ruby. Her chicken
is crisp, well done and beautiful to behold. I think she dis-
joints her bird, salts and peppers the pieces and rolls them in
flour and cooks them slowly in the time-honored way, parting
company with other cooks only in using ½ olive oil and ½
cooking oil for frying. This is not deep fat, which roadside
chicken places are prone to use until it tastes like old crank-
case oil, but about ½ inch in an iron skillet.

IRON POT CHICKEN

When having out-of-door parties and cooking chicken for
twenty-five or thirty people, we have swung an iron pot from
a tripod over a small controlled fire and used deep fat.
Chicken pieces are rubbed with salt and pepper and rolled
in flour the usual way and added a few at a time to the cooking oil, which should be hot, rolling slightly but not smoking.
The advantage here is that when a piece of chicken is cooked

through it floats to the top of the kettle and you lift it off in a wire basket and drain it either in the basket or on paper towels.

BARBECUED CHICKEN

On summer evenings when friends come out from town we sometimes set up wire racks over a bed of charcoal at the edge of the terrace and cook chicken there. Broilers are best for this, allowing half a chicken for each serving. I precook the chicken in the house in an iron skillet, seasoning it with salt, pepper and melted butter or margarine. When it is tender I transfer it to a mammoth crockery baking dish I have and cover it with a sauce made up of 1 part ketchup, 1 vinegar, 1 mustard with a seasoning of brown sugar, Worcestershire sauce and a few tablespoons of lemon juice. After it has been laved in this sauce for an hour or so the chicken is ready to go to the terrace and be browned over the coals.

So impressed was Jack with charcoal-broiled chicken cooked by the 4-H Club girls and Home Demonstration Clubs at the annual Rich's harvest curb market that he begged their recipe. They cook hundreds of chickens over a sidewalk fire and because of the size of the operation squirt their marinade on the birds from a garden sprayer with pressurized nozzle. The marinade consists of melted butter and lemon juice but they recommended a Wish-Bone Dressing that comes in a bottle to Jack and he likes it just as well. He does not precook his chicken but makes sure that he has a very low fire, cooking the chicken slowly—an hour or more. (So far he hasn't cooked chicken in sufficient quantity to warrant the purchase of a pressurized garden spray for the dressing.)

JULIA'S BROWN CHICKEN STEW

Fryer—3 to 4 pounds
1 medium onion
2 cloves garlic
1 heaping cooking spoon flour
¼ cup corn oil
1 tablespoon chopped green onions
1 tablespoon chopped parsley

Heat 1 tablespoon corn oil in a 6-quart heavy pot. Salt and pepper pieces of chicken and brown in oil. (Need not be too brown.) Add 6 cups water and simmer. Meanwhile, in an iron skillet make a roux of ¼ cup corn oil and flour, stirring constantly to keep smooth. Roux should be medium brown. Add onion and garlic and cook about 3 minutes, stirring constantly. Add to chicken pot and cook about an hour or until chicken is tender and gravy is desired thickness. Add parsley and green onions just before serving over steamed rice.

BRUNSWICK STEW

When Maude and Erle Miles have an outdoor party for very special guests they sometimes perform that labor of love known as Brunswick Stew. The recipe is an old one from Erle's family in North Carolina and to my notion is more felicitously prepared by a staff of colored cooks. However, in these servantless days the Mileses do the whole chore themselves with Erle meticulously directing the mammoth operation, which can run into two days.

They start the stew the day before the party by boiling what their old hand-written recipe calls "three nice hens" until the meat falls from the bones. Remove bones and reserve chicken broth. The next day transfer meat to an iron pot over coals in the yard. Cook 2 pounds of fat bacon which has been ground. Put in chicken broth. As this cooks begin adding vegetables by easy progression, always stirring and cooking awhile before each new batch. The vegetables: 5 pounds chopped onions, 2 pounds sliced Irish potatoes, 2 gallons canned tomatoes, 1 gallon tomato puree, 2 gallons creamed corn. The last addition, just before serving, is a pound of country butter. Seasoning is to taste—a little sugar, salt and a pod of red pepper.

The day the stew is served Erle stands over the pot, stirring with a wooden paddle from 8 a.m. until 4 p.m., at which time guests gather on the lawn and Maude begins setting out bowls and spoons and great green mounds of cole slaw, which with bread is all you need to share the attention better concentrated on the fragrant main dish—the stew.

Leftover stew, if any, can be frozen in quart containers and used as an occasion for a party weeks or months later.

STEAK

Steak at Sweet Apple bespeaks a festive occasion of the first order. In winter we make a ritual of cooking it over hickory coals on the hearth. (Wood coals haven't the oily smell of charcoal and we think add superior flavor.) In summer, however, to avoid the heat of a full-fledged wood fire we make do with charcoal on the terrace, simply adding a few hickory twigs for flavor. The green leaves are as efficacious as hickory chips.

Just as Charles Lamb's people accidentally learned the joys of roast pig when the house burned down, I learned of chuck steak when Jimmy, about to be a bridegroom, confused the best sirloin with a cheap chuck roast. I left directions for him to cook the roast in foil with dehydrated onion soup for his lunch, while I went off to a tea for Marie, his bride-to-be. When I came home Jimmy had given a five-dollar steak, bought for special company, the cheap onion soup treatment, cooked it within an inch of its life and served it to himself and some workmen. I had the coals on the hearth ready before I discovered the switch. The company was in the living room and I stood in the kitchen with the cheap tough hunk of chuck in my hands ready to cry when Doc saved the day.

"Chuck's fine," he said. "Better flavored than sirloin sometimes. We'll just take out some of the coals and cook it more slowly. It'll be good, you'll see."

It was delicious.

Since then we have refined the preparation somewhat, taking the chuck out of the refrigerator a couple of hours before dinnertime, sprinkling it well with meat tenderizer and marinating it with garlic juice, Worcestershire sauce and sometimes wine. Once I heard a Negro cook at the meat counter at the A & P advise a young bride to marinate cheap meat in a little bourbon and I have tried that with some success. If you want gravy for your potatoes, the marinade, thickened with a bit of browned flour and flavored with meat juice, is very tasty.

For purists the thick sirloin, cooked over the coals and then salted, is the be-all and end-all of steaks and to do more to one is an offense against this aristocrat of meats. I'm sorry but I like to putter around a bit with garlic (again use the press) and coarsely ground black pepper. We recently started coating the steak well with cracked peppercorns, after seeing a picture in *Life* magazine, cooking it in a bit of suet in a skillet on top of the stove and found it a wondrous change indeed.

One warning: Keep the peppercorns coarse. If you grind them fine the steak will be so hot you can hardly eat it.

(Incidentally, although I'm squinchy about buying most kitchen equipment I think a really good pepper mill is a worthy investment. The fancy giant ones of wood don't stand up to much wear but a small utilitarian metal one made in France promises to be worth its weight in gold. I bought it after reading a querulous statement by an old cook that store-bought, ready-ground pepper wasn't fit for human consumption.)

It's more festive to broil steaks over coals, either in the fireplace or the yard, but sometimes we haven't the time to wait for the fire to burn low enough. Then we broil them on top of the stove with happy results. Again cut a bit of suet from the steak or ask your butcher to give you an extra piece or two, grease your iron skillet well and plunk your steak in when it is hot. If the steak is a couple of inches thick and you want it rare, cook about 8 minutes to the side. (I inherited from Muv an unawareness of time and I usually have to take the steak off the fire and cut into it near the bone to be sure, returning it to the fire if it is too rare.)

BEEF

Jack sometimes cooks an extraordinarily juicy, tender rib roast, saving the juice for Yorkshire pudding. Far from taking credit for any culinary originality, he says the recipe is one he read in a magazine at the barbershop some years ago. As close as I can come to this triumph is this:

Preheat oven to 300 degrees. Place the roast, fat side up, in an uncovered roasting pan. Salt and pepper. Roast 18 to 20 minutes per pound for rare roast, longer for medium and well done. The slow heat keeps the meat from shrinking and gradually brings out the juices which are a must if you're to have Yorkshire pudding.

YORKSHIRE PUDDING

Preheat oven to 450 degrees. Mix together 1 cup milk, 1 cup flour, ¼ teaspoon salt. Add 2 slightly beaten eggs and beat well. Pour meat juice into a shallow bread pan and re-heat. Pour batter on top of the juice to a thickness of about ¼ inch. Bake until brown and puffy. Cut into squares and serve with roast. It will be well seasoned with the gravy.

The same open pan method is the one we use on almost all roasts. A corner-cut rump, outside tip, which is my favorite for tender, close-grained meat that slices beautifully for sandwiches, has but to have a whiff of garlic patted into it along with salt and pepper before you put it in the oven, fat side up. (A meat thermometer helps you feel secure about not overcooking it.) Chuck cooked in onion soup and foil is a busy-day standby and cheap.

BEEF STEW

Julia buys chuck for stew and has it cut into chunks about 2 inches square, flouring and browning, seasoning with garlic and making a roux of the meat juices, bacon drippings and flour as a base before returning the meat to the pot and adding vegetables.

MEAT PIE

When my children were small and the budget seldom allowed a Sunday roast I Sundayfied what was then cheap stew meat by making a meat pie of it. We still like it. The basic method used by Julia is good here for cooking the meat, except that for pie I cut the stew meat into smaller, bite-size pieces. Flour and brown them in fat, in which a clove of garlic is sautéed. While the browned meat drains on paper sauté a couple of onions, a bell pepper and celery chopped fine. When this is cooked through but not brown, remove from fat and stir in a couple of tablespoons of flour, brown well, add about 2 cups of hot water, enough to make plenty of gravy. Return meat, onions, pepper and celery to pot and simmer gently while you peel and dice 4 potatoes and 4 or 5 carrots. Add these to the pot and cook until tender. It might be necessary to add water to have plenty of gravy and if I have leftover English peas or tomatoes I fling them in. A few mushrooms are a real flossy touch.

When all this is done, cool slightly (or cook the night before and cool completely, if you want to) and line a big baking dish with pie crust, reserving enough dough for an upper crust. Pour in stew, apply top crust and bake in a 375-degree oven 30 or 40 minutes, until the crust is brown.

A green salad and a dessert helped this old meat pie see us through not only Sunday dinners but was useful in filling up hungry guests on many occasions. Garnished with a sprig of parsley and brought to the table in a baking dish set in a basket, it looks respectable enough for any occasion.

Since I have never mastered the light touch with pie crust I turn to mixes for this, finding the cheapest as good as the most expensive for some reason. They are probably more expensive, at that, than home-mixed pie crust but they're terribly handy when you're in a hurry.

As a variation on the stew theme, I sometimes leave out the potatoes, add a small can of English peas to the foregoing mixture and omit the pie crust, embellishing this plain workaday fare as follows:

1.   Spoon cooked hot rice into a round mold, which has been buttered lightly. Turn rice out on a platter. Fill center with stew.

2.   Put stew in my best deep platter, spoon hot mashed potatoes in a sort of feathery circle around it, dust with paprika and ornament with parsley. If the stew is so soupy

it threatens to encroach on the potatoes or rice, drain off most of the gravy and serve separately.

CORNED BEEF WITH MACARONI

One of our favorite cheapy-quickies was evolved by Muv when our staples came out of a turpentine still-sawmill commissary, which my father ran for his uncle. When fresh vegetables and meat were in short supply or she was in a hurry Muv would send me to the commissary for a can of corned beef (then 15 cents) and she would whip up a dish that still rates high in our family affections.

She began by sautéeing onions, a finely chopped clove of garlic and a bell pepper, if she had one, in a little bacon fat in an iron skillet. (Sometimes now I use olive oil instead of bacon fat for a subtly different flavor.) To this she added corned beef pulled apart with a fork. When this has cooked a minute or two add a can of tomatoes, cover and let it all simmer while a package of elbow macaroni cooks in another pot. When the macaroni is tender, drain, blanch and add to the beef-tomato mixture.

Keep hot until the flavor of the sauce has permeated the macaroni or until you have finished your washing and ironing. A little grated parmesan cheese is a pleasant addition to this dish that I've picked up in recent years. With a salad and hot French bread company won't snoot it.

Among our more interesting neighbors in the north end of Fulton County are Wilma Van Dusseldorf and Fern Maddox, a couple of ex-social workers, ex-school teachers, who quit their jobs, left the city behind them and moved to the woods to start an herb farm. Miss Van bought some poor pineland along Big Creek back in the 1930s with the idea of someday restoring it to fertility and productivity. A few years after World War II she and her partner, Miss Maddox, decided to give it a try.

Fern was interested in raising animals and they started by building a small modern barn to house their cows. Before it was finished they decided to move into it themselves and they are still there with greenhouse, potting shed, studio and office marching along the slope beside them. Fern gave up on cows after a trial or two, and now raises sheep, rabbits and bantam chickens for their own use.

Miss Van raises herbs which she ships to all parts of the country. And when she is not growing or shipping herbs she is experimenting with herb cookery. I was at Pine Hills Herb Farm one day and without departing the conversation for a moment, Miss Van moved lightly around the pleasant little kitchen lifting a lid on a pot, stirring and mixing. Within moments she set before us a memorable lunch.

I begged her recipe for scallop and leek soup, along with some others which owe their individuality to herbs.

SCALLOP AND LEEK SOUP

5 or 6 spears of leek, depending upon size
2 cups boiling water
2 cups shredded cooked scallops
2 cups stock in which scallops were cooked

4 tablespoons soy sauce
1 cup canned milk
4 tablespoons minced parsley

Cut spears of leek into ¼ inch slices and cover with boiling water. Place on high heat until mixture boils vigorously. Then reduce to medium heat and cook until leek is tender, which takes only a few minutes. Add shredded scallops, scallop stock, soy sauce and milk and reduce heat to simmer. When mixture is thoroughly heated, serve, sprinkling parsley over each serving.

HERB SALAD

1 medium head of cabbage, white or red, or mixture of both
1 medium white onion
1 grapefruit
3 tablespoons herb vinegar (we use basil)
3 tablespoons salad dressing
2 cups finely minced herbs such as parsley, sorrel, oregano, sweet marjoram, garlic, chives, burnet, rose geranium, lovage or smallage, upland cress, pepper grass and thyme. Any two or three or all may be used—green

Shred or chop cabbage in large mixing bowl. Add finely minced onion, herbs, sections of grapefruit, vinegar and salad dressing. Mix thoroughly. Serve on lettuce leaves or finely shredded greens such as curly or plain endive.

DILL BREAD

1 package dry yeast
1 tablespoon honey
1 cup cottage cheese
1 tablespoon minced onion
1 tablespoon butter
2 teaspoons dill seed
1 teaspoon salt
¼ teaspoon baking soda
1 unbeaten egg
2¼ or 2½ cups whole wheat flour
¼ cup warm water

Soften yeast in warm water; heat cottage cheese until warm, then add honey, butter, onion, salt, soda, dill seed, softened yeast and unbeaten egg. Stir well. Add flour sufficient to make stiff dough. Let dough rise in warm place until double in bulk, then work down and make into loaves and put in warm place for 40 minutes or longer if necessary. Bake in 350-degree preheated oven until well done (approximately 40 minutes).

Although I visit Pine Hills Herb Farm and come home with the back seat of my car smelling divinely of lavender and thyme and pennyroyal and rose geranium I still haven't the full-fledged herb garden I dream of.

Mary (Mrs. David) Kistner, another city woman turned farmer, planned me one with formal little paths and everything tidy and traditional the way an herb garden should be. But so far I have two or three kinds of mint spilling over the terrace wall like a boisterous waterfall, chives and garlic popping up in the tomato bed and catnip elbowing the asparagus out of the way. It's all I can do to remember where I stuck the parsley when I'm in a hurry for a sprig or two. (My neighbor, Mrs. Stiles, has a more formal informal method. She always scatters a package of parsley seed among her hollyhocks and petunias.)

Considering that I didn't care for it much in the first place and it always disappoints me in the garden I've put in some time cooking eggplant. Jack Spalding, who gardens a bit at Sandy Springs, told me I couldn't go wrong with eggplant. He remembered from travels around the Mediterranean that it thrives on hot rocky soil and neglect. So every year I plant eggplant, see it die, and then go buy some at the market because it's so beautiful to look at and because, willy nilly, I've learned to cook it so it tastes like something.

BAKED EGGPLANT

Parboil the beauty about 5 or 6 minutes in salted water, cool, cut a thin slice off one side and scoop out as much of its insides as you can without disturbing the shell. Chop up the meat of the eggplant and sauté in a skillet with butter, 1 medium chopped onion and 2 small chopped tomatoes. Season with salt and pepper, return to eggplant shell, top with butter and bread crumbs and bake for 20 minutes.

Sometimes I vary this a bit by mixing a beaten egg with the stuffing after it has cooled enough not to cook the egg.

Sometimes I sauté hamburger meat and mix with the stuffing. Bits of crisply fried bacon give it still another flavor. In fact, I think I've tried everything but ice cream in eggplant —with the result that it has become one of our favorite dishes.

I still think anything else—paper, sponge, potato peelings— tastes as well fried so I won't offer any fried eggplant recipes here.

When you need a vegetable and haven't anything inspiring in the house, baked stuffed onions are good and look pretty ranged around steak or roast on a platter.

BAKED STUFFED ONIONS

Parboil 6 or 8 medium onions in salted water until they are tender but retain their shape. Cool. Scoop out and chop insides, leaving a couple of layers on each onion to form a shell. Mix a cupful of seasoned bread crumbs (the kind they sell for turkey stuffing) with half a stick of butter and a cup of hot water. Add chopped onions, mix and return to shells. Top with a lump of butter and bake in a 350-degree oven for 15 minutes, until brown and cooked through.

Our friend Fred Williams was a premier fisherman before he died a few years ago and like most outdoorsmen he could throw together a good meal with a minimum of trouble. His pressure cooker corn is a favorite of ours.

FRED'S CORN

4 ears corn
3 slices bacon
1 tablespoon butter or oleo
¼ cup water
Salt, pepper

Clean corn, fry bacon in pressure cooker. Pour off fat. Add butter, salt and pepper and water. Add corn. Pressure cook 2 minutes. Cool pot fast under water. Serve at once.

When the corn is young and tender there's really no better way than to cook it in the husks, pulling them back first to remove the silk and be sure there are no worms. Then replace the husk, wrap the ear in foil and roast it on the coals over the grill, in the ashes on the hearth or in the oven, if that's more convenient. Serve with salt, pepper and butter and let each person season his own.

Creamed corn, freshly cut from the cob, and cooked slowly with a bit of cream, salt and pepper, is a dish we enjoy when Muv is at Sweet Apple to cook it. The task of cutting the corn from the cob is so time-consuming I seldom get around to it. Besides that, you have to stand over it and stir it to keep it from scorching.

Easier but, of course, not nearly so good is corn soufflé made from canned corn.

CORN SOUFFLE

1 large can corn
2 cups milk
3 eggs
3 tablespoons melted butter
1 teaspoon salt
1 teaspoon sugar
1 tablespoon cornstarch

Drain corn in a colander. Transfer to mixing bowl. Dissolve cornstarch in milk and stir into corn along with sugar and salt and the eggs, well beaten. Add melted butter. Pour into casserole and bake at 375 degrees about 40 minutes.

CABBAGE

Cabbage grows well around Sweet Apple and although I don't have it in my garden it's not unusual to come home and find a green head, looking like a mammoth rose, on the back porch where some neighbor has left it.

It's hard to improve on cutting it into wedges, cooking it in the pressure cooker 5 minutes and serving it up with butter, salt and pepper.

But there is a way I watched my young friend Laura Barre cook cabbage years ago. I didn't ask for her recipe and I may have improvised on the theme but we like it and have it often.

CABBAGE A LA BARRE

Sauté 1 medium onion, chopped, and 1 bell pepper, chopped, in half a stick of melted margarine or butter in Dutch oven. Wash and chop medium head of cabbage and add to the pot with only the water which clings to the leaves. Stir until well wilted. (It will have moisture enough within a minute or two.) As the cabbage cooks down cut 2 tomatoes into wedges and add. More butter may be added along with salt and freshly ground pepper. When cabbage is tender and tomatoes are cooked, serve. This shouldn't take more than 15 minutes.

My doctor, William R. Crowe, is both a gardener and a cook and he came up with practically the same recipe, using just onions and cabbage and crisp crumbled bacon.

From Verda we picked up the custom of having corned beef on the weekends, when there is time to simmer it long and well. When the beef is almost done (we buy the kind that comes in a plastic bag in brine and follow the directions), we add wedges of cabbage, half a dozen whole potatoes, onions and carrots. Turn out the beef on a platter, slice, arrange vegetables around it and sprinkle with a little chopped parsley.

Among the old country artifacts I have hanging on my wall is a long-handled sauerkraut chopper with a curved, home-made blade. (I also have a buggywhip holder, a harness maker's vise, a shoemaker's last and a few other such treasures hanging where I can see them. My pleasure in them prompted

Olivia to tell Clarence when he cleaned out one of their sheds to bring the overflow to me. "Celestine will hang *anything* on her walls!") So far the sauerkraut cutter has been more of an art object than a kitchen tool because I haven't had to make any sauerkraut myself. All my neighbors make it and are very generous about sharing it. Some of them still pack it down in crocks, as in the old days, but both Verda and Olivia now seal it in fruit jars.

VERDA'S SAUERKRAUT

Wash cabbage, shred it fine and pack in fruit jars, adding a teaspoon of salt to each quart of cabbage. Fill jars with boiling water, tighten lids and seal. You can use cold water, Verda tells me, and let the jars stand four days before sealing. Either way the result is "clear" kraut.

With sauerkraut Verda sometimes serves frankfurters but one of her more enticing dishes is sauerkraut with ribs. She seasons the ribs and browns them, then tops a baking dish of sauerkraut with them, popping them into a medium oven until the ribs are tender.

Having been reared on the coast it was difficult for me, when I moved to Atlanta, to accept the fact that fish so far inland could be fresh. Refrigeration and fast shipping methods are all very well but when you are accustomed to seeing your fish kicking, it's hard to believe anything reposing on a bed of ice in a glass showcase is the same vintage. Julia, who lives on the coast with a husband who fishes almost daily, usually has so many fish she has to freeze some of them and she has put me on to a method of keeping our local fresh-water catches.

A gallon plastic milk carton with its top cut off makes a handy container. You pack numbers of cleaned bream and bass in it, cover them with water and freeze. The important thing is to have the fish immersed in water, Julia says. When you thaw and dry them before preparing them they are as fresh as they were when you took them from the stream.

When choosing your fish at the market, Julia says, make sure that the gills are pink or red, the meat firm, not mushy or soft. Those we thaw from our iced cartons always pass the test in addition to curling a little when they hit the hot grease.

Julia's baked red fish or red snapper is something to remember and well worth the trouble.

JULIA'S BAKED FISH

1 3½- or 4-pound red fish or snapper
½ teaspoon salt
½ teaspoon pepper
3 slices bacon
1 lemon, sliced

Sauce

1 large onion, chopped
2 stalks celery, chopped
2 cloves garlic, minced
¼ cup chopped green pepper
2 sprigs parsley, chopped fine

2 tablespoons corn oil
1 1-pound can whole tomatoes
1 8-ounce can tomato sauce
Salt and pepper to taste

Sauté onion, celery, green pepper and garlic in corn oil until transparent. Add tomatoes, tomato sauce, salt and pepper. Bring to a boil. Simmer slowly, covered, about 2 hours.

Score fish crosswise twice. Salt and pepper well. Place in greased baking dish, put bacon and sliced lemon on top. Bake in 350-degree oven 20 minutes. Add sauce, bake 45 minutes or an hour longer, until fish flakes easily when touched with a fork. Just before serving sprinkle with chopped parsley.

For years shrimp gumbo was one of my company recipes and then I lucked into Julia's shrimp and crab gumbo recipe which is even more of a good thing. Its secret, I believe, is the roux, dark and rich and of creamy consistency. I made it for my shrimp gumbo but Julia uses it for a great many of her fragrant, spicy "pots"—shrimp and crab gumbo, chicken stew and duck and turnips. Her basic recipe for

ROUX

¼ cup corn oil or meat drippings
⅔ cup plain flour
1 medium onion, chopped
2 cloves garlic, chopped fine

Heat oil in heavy skillet, add flour, stir until brown. Add onion and garlic. Cook about 2 minutes.

SHRIMP, CRAB, OKRA GUMBO

1½ pounds cleaned and deveined shrimp
½ dozen fresh crabs, cleaned and cracked
½ pound okra, chopped
¼ cup corn oil
1 medium onion
2 cloves garlic, chopped
¼ pound ham, chopped
1 teaspoon Ac'cent
7 cups water
Salt and pepper to taste

Heat oil in Dutch oven, add okra, onion, ham and garlic. Cook over low fire until okra won't rope. Add water, salt, pepper and Ac'cent. Make roux, omitting onion and garlic since you have already added them to the vegetable mixture. Cook 1 hour. Sauté shrimp and crabs in oil in a heavy skillet a few minutes and add to vegetables. Cook about 20 minutes. Serve over rice. (Omit ham on days of abstinence, Julia advises.)

(My shrimp gumbo recipe varies little except that I boil the cleaned, deveined shrimp separately, using the water in which they are cooked in the gumbo. And if I can get them

I sometimes use small whole pods of okra instead of cut okra.)

Julia's chicken gumbo with filé is called "Christmas Gumbo" in her family and it's an inspired thing to have around during the Christmas season when you want something hot and nourishing.

CHICKEN GUMBO FILE OR CHRISTMAS GUMBO

>   1 frying-size chicken, cut up
>   ¼ cup corn oil
>   ¼ pound ham
>   1 pint oysters
>   7 cups water
>   ½ teaspoon filé (pulverized sassafras leaves)
>   1 teaspoon Ac'cent
>   1 tablespoon chopped parsley
>   2 tablespoons chopped green onion
>   Salt and pepper to taste

Salt and pepper chicken. Fry a few minutes in corn oil (need not brown). Dice ham and sauté. Put chicken in heavy Dutch oven with water. When chicken is tender add ham and Ac'cent. Ten minutes before serving add oysters. Remove from fire and add filé. Let stand a few minutes, add parsley and green onion before serving over steamed rice.

Julia applies the same treatment to the succulent wild ducks which are plentiful in the marshes along the Pearl

River, where the Morrises spend many a weekend. The duck is disjointed and sautéed, just as in her stewed chicken recipe mentioned earlier. The roux is made the same but the vegetables added are surprising—turnips. About 20 minutes before the duck, bathed in brown gravy, is ready to serve, Julia adds 4 medium turnips, peeled and halved.

Perhaps the most filling sumptuous one-dish meal to be brought up from the Gulf Coast is that Creole specialty jambalaya (pronounced jumble-lie).

This, too, is Julia's recipe:

JAMBALAYA

8 crabs or 1½ pounds shrimp (cleaned and deveined)
1 pound ham, chopped, or smoked sausage
Salt and pepper to taste
¼ cup corn oil
1½ cups raw rice
1 medium onion
1 stalk celery
2 cloves garlic, minced
¼ cup chopped green pepper
2 cups water
1 teaspoon Ac'cent
2 tablespoons chopped green onions
1 tablespoon minced parsley

Heat oil in a 4- or 6-quart Dutch oven. Add onion and celery and sauté until transparent. If using ham sauté along with onion and celery. Add rice, stir and fry about 5 minutes. Add shrimp or crabs or sausage. Cook a few minutes. Add green pepper, green onions, garlic and parsley, salt and pepper and Ac'cent. Let boil ½ hour, adding small amount of boiling water, if necessary, or until the rice is tender. Serve hot.

Country hams are still to be had around Sweet Apple, both home-grown and boughten. If you buy one in the market it is more than likely from Talmadge Farm, where Betty, wife of U. S. Senator Herman Talmadge, has run an old country recipe for curing hams into a thriving business. These hams come high and are greatly prized by visitors from afar. I happened to be present when the Talmadges were in the governor's mansion in Atlanta and Betty presented a guest named Adlai Stevenson one of her hams with full directions for cooking it.

She told me later that she had a note from Mr. Stevenson which indicated that the gentleman from Illinois had taken to Georgia country ham as if raised on red-eye gravy.

(Just recently I read in that marvelous volume *Bull Cook and Authentic Historical Recipes and Practices* that red-eye gravy was given its name by General Andrew Jackson. It seems that Old Hickory had a cook who, as we say, "took whiskey" and as a result was often red-eyed at breakfast time. The general is supposed to have told him to bring him some ham with gravy "as red as your eyes." Overhearing it, soldiers took up the name, as soldiers will, and it has come down through the years to designate the hot meat juice, which is left in the skillet after frying ham.)

Not all people like country ham. It is strong meat, often salty and sometimes tough. Mr. Tabor quotes a mountain authority who smokes his own as saying it ought to be against the law to cut into one of the black-crusted hams before it is four years old.

If you happen to like country ham and are so fortunate as to get a really good one, Maude Miles has an old and prized recipe for cooking it.

MAUDE'S BAKED HAM

Soak ham overnight and put on to boil the next morning. Add 1 cup of black cooking molasses and 1 pint of vinegar. Boil 20 minutes to the pound. Cool in the same liquid. Remove skin when cool and trim off any excess fat. Sprinkle bread crumbs on the ham and rub into it. Score and stud with allspice or cloves. Place in a 300-degree oven and bake until done, basting occasionally with Coca-Cola if you like.

While we're on the subject of pork, Maude makes marvelous pickled pig feet. Crabapple Sausage Company, a small packing house near us, frequently has them for sale and Maude will buy two dozen pig feet at a time.

PICKLED PIG FEET

Boil pig feet in plenty of salted water until tender. Drain. To 1½ quarts vinegar (she uses cider vinegar) add 1 dozen each whole cloves, allspice and peppercorns. Bring to a boil, pour over pig feet. Let stand overnight.

For years I wondered why country sausage wasn't as good as I remembered it from childhood when my Great Aunt Babe always gave it to us. She made her own, seasoning with herbs out of her garden, shaping it into patties, which she cooked and packed down in fruit jars filled with hot grease to keep it through the winter. I had about attributed my disappointment in present-day sausage to the prejudice and possibly the superior digestive equipment of childhood, when I happened to breakfast with the Tabors one winter morning.

Along with hot biscuits and grits Frances served the best country sausage I had eaten since Aunt Babe's. The secret lay in an old recipe which has been in the Tabor family for probably a hundred years or more. Frances buys the sausage makings at the market and has them ground to her specifications, doing the seasoning herself.

TABOR SAUSAGE

12 pounds of pork shoulder, 8 lean, 4 fat
2 tablespoons salt
2 tablespoons red pepper
1 tablespoon sage

Have the butcher trim the shoulder and grind once. Season and grind again. Frances freezes the sausage in small lots and brings it out before she is

ready to shape it into patties, brown it quickly, add
a little hot water, cover and simmer until done.

The natural accompaniment for sausage or ham is, of
course, hot biscuits. For a party we make the biscuits and the
sausage patties small—about bite size—taking the biscuits from
the oven, breaking them in the middle, sticking a sausage
patty in them and serving them immediately. Ham and hot
biscuits are wonderful hors d'oeuvres. Thinly slice enough of
the ham to start the guests off and then they will take over
and serve themselves and all you have to do is have a relay
system for running biscuits from the kitchen as fast as they
come out of the oven.

In this, the hot bread belt, it is considered unpardonable
to serve a guest a cold biscuit. There's an old story, probably
apocryphal, of the northern visitor who spent months in the
South and never got to taste biscuits because every time he
would reach for one his hostesses would cry, "Let me get you a
hot one!" and snatch them away.

That might very well have happened in the Jarrett House
in Ellijay, an old-time mountain boardinghouse famous for
its food. Miss Kitty Jarrett, one of the granddaughters of the
founder, who with her sisters ran it until their recent retire-
ment, circulated around the table with a plate of hot biscuits,
making frequent runs to the big wood stove in the kitchen.
The Jarretts are good company and I wondered once why
Miss Kitty would never pull up a chair and sit with us.

"Oh, she wouldn't put the biscuits down!" somebody explained.

It was true I had never seen a plate of biscuits stationary

on that laden table and I learned that Miss Kitty not only eschewed the practice of having biscuits wait on the diners, she eschewed diners who caused the biscuits to wait. City people driving through the mountains often tried to reach Ellijay at mealtime but if they got there five or ten minutes late Miss Kitty wouldn't admit them to the table.

"I'm not serving cold biscuits to *anybody!*" she said.

The Jarretts grew their own vegetables, raised their own meats and cooked on a wood stove until the day they stopped taking boarders. City water comes to the big white two-story house by the railroad tracks but they still have a pipe running from the spring on the hillside out back, bringing in cold sweet "natural" water for coffee.

My own biscuits, which Muv started me to making when I was eight or nine years old, were a matter of pride with me until my ungrateful children once asked if we couldn't have canned biscuits "like other people." It was a real case of casting pearls before swine, I thought, wounded. But I bought some canned ones and liked them fine. Now I only make biscuits if I'm out of canned ones or am having a party and want little cocktail-sized biscuits.

There are two kinds—the light fluffy ones and the short ones. The ingredients vary slightly.

FLUFFY BISCUITS

2 cups flour
5 teaspoons baking powder
2 tablespoons shortening
1 cup milk
½ teaspoon salt

Sift dry ingredients together twice. Cut shortening in with a pastry blender or the fingers. Add milk gradually, working it in, roll dough to thickness of about half an inch, handling it lightly. Cut with small cutter, jar lid or glass, place in 400-degree oven and bake about 12 minutes.

SHORT BISCUITS

2 cups flour
4 teaspoons baking powder
¾ teaspoon salt
6 tablespoons shortening
¾ cup milk

Sift dry ingredients, as for fluffy biscuits. Work in shortening until the flour is mealy. Add milk, turn out on a floured board and roll out to a thickness of about half an inch. Cut and cook in a very hot oven, 450 degrees, for about 10 minutes.

A few years ago a vogue for "riz biscuits," which are biscuits with yeast, swept over Georgia and the recipe was handed from cook to cook all over the state. Mine came to me from Frances. I don't know who the real mother of this marvelously light bread is but generations will be indebted to her.

RIZ BISCUITS

2½ cups flour
4 tablespoons shortening
1 teaspoon baking powder
1 teaspoon salt
½ teaspoon baking soda
1 tablespoon sugar
½ package yeast
1 cup buttermilk

Sift together dry ingredients. Cut in shortening. Dissolve yeast in buttermilk, which should be at room temperature. Stir into flour mixture and roll out very thin, not more than a quarter of an inch, on a floured board. Cut, butter tops and place one biscuit on top of another in buttery twosomes. Place in warm spot to rise for about an hour before baking in a hot oven.

From Frances I also have another light bread recipe appropriately named:

ANGEL BISCUITS

5 cups flour to start; it may take more for a stiff dough
¼ to ⅓ cup sugar
1 teaspoon baking soda

3 teaspoons baking powder
1 package yeast dissolved in ¼ cup warm water
1 cup shortening
2 cups buttermilk at room temperature

Combine dry ingredients, cut in shortening and stir in yeast and milk. Roll and cut as desired. Bake in middle rack of oven at 450 degrees for 12 to 14 minutes or till brown. Dough may be covered and refrigerated as long as a week, using as needed.

Frances makes hot rolls with less to-do than anybody I ever saw. Once while vacationing at Holly Creek we arrived at the Tabor house in the late afternoon to put a young guest, Margaret Leonard, on the bus for Atlanta. The bus was late and Frances said it was imperative that we feed the child before sending her forth. The Tabors had eaten their dinner at mid-day but there was plenty of cold sliced roast, Frances said, and she was just going to pop some rolls into the oven. The young people, six or eight strong, pulled up chairs in the Tabor kitchen and as fast as Frances brought the rolls out of the oven they vanished—along with mounds of country butter and several jars of honey and homemade jams and jellies.

I was busy eating and didn't notice the progress of my progeny and friends until out of a happy silence, broken only by the sound of the butter dish being passed, I heard Margaret say to Jimmy: "You know how many rolls you've eaten? I've kept count—fourteen!"

FRANCES' ROLLS

1 package yeast
1 quart milk
1 cup sugar
1 cup lard

Mix yeast in ½ cup of tepid water. Add to above. Add enough sifted flour to make a stiff batter. (You're on your own here. I guess about 4 or 5 cups.) Let rise 2 hours. Work down and add:

5 teaspoons baking powder
3 teaspoons salt
1 teaspoon sugar

Add flour to make dough. (Several cups, says Frances.) Roll out on floured board, cut into rounds and let rise 20 to 30 minutes. Or if you want to, put in refrigerator and bring out and let rise another day, as when a swarm of hungry children descend on you.

Desserts are a seasonal thing at Sweet Apple. Weeks pass and I don't think of making a goodie of any kind, except possibly to stir up a packaged pudding if the babies are going to be out, or to take a package of vanilla ice cream out of the freezer and serve it with store-bought cookies. But when the little wild strawberries start ripening in May we can't get enough of them. They are small, fun to pick but tedious to hull and well worth every minute of trouble.

The heedless modern custom of using sponge cake or those little sweet packaged sponge cups instead of truly *short* shortcake would be an insult to these wonderful little berries. So I always make a crisp biscuit dough, bake it in a sheet, butter it well, cut it in half, sprinkle sugar on it and make two layers, united by a heavenly mixture of slightly mashed, slightly sweetened strawberries. Thick yellow cream is the natural topping but whipped cream very sparingly sweetened is not to be sneezed at.

Cold biscuits, split, buttered and toasted make equally good individual shortcakes. Sprinkle a little sugar over them as you bring them out of the oven, rush the strawberries between the layers and serve while the biscuit is still hot and very crisp. Oh, my.

Ruby Chadwick has earned considerable fame in the settlement with her strawberry pie, which is much sought after at church meetings and reunions.

RUBY'S STRAWBERRY PIE

1 quart berries
1 cup sugar
4 tablespoons cornstarch
1 cup whipping cream
1 baked pie shell

Line pie shell with one pint of whole berries, putting the stem sides down. Mash the other pint of berries. Combine the sugar with cornstarch and stir into the mashed berries, bringing them to a boil and cooking about 3 minutes. Berries should be the consistency of jelly when cool. Pour over uncooked berries in pie shell while hot and let cool before covering with whipped cream. Ruby does not sweeten her whipped cream.

Apple season is another time for desserts at Sweet Apple. The big June apple tree in the back yard is such a good provider I find myself making applesauce, apple pies, apple cobbler and baked apples at a dead gallop for the weeks the apples are at their prime. These particular apples do not keep well so it's a matter of now or never.

Apple pie, which I make about the same as everybody else, is one of the world's most satisfying desserts, I think. (You know the routine: plenty of apples, cored, sliced, sweetened, generously daubed with butter, dusted with nutmeg and enveloped top and bottom in pie crust.) A piece of cheese cut from the big hoop on Chadwick's counter is the natural entremets to this simple old-fashioned apple pie or its sister, deep dish apple cobbler.

But on a cold winter night when you're having soup for supper, there's nothing quite up to Muv's apple dumplings.

MUV'S APPLE DUMPLINGS

> 2 cups chopped tart apples
> 1 cup sugar
> 1 stick butter
> Nutmeg

Make a short rich pastry, cut in four-inch rounds. In the center of each round put a generous mound of finely chopped apples, butter, sugar and a dash of nutmeg. Bring edges of the pastry together over the apple mixture and pinch securely. Place in baking dish and brown. Make a sauce of rich milk, sugar and butter and a dash of nutmeg and pour over the dumplings. (Muv doesn't measure but they should be if not *swimming* at least *wading* in the sauce.) Return to oven and keep hot until time to serve.

There are those who extol cinnamon as the proper spice for apple pie and apple dumplings but we are members of the nutmeg school. However, Frances makes an orange-apple pie which employs cinnamon, and magnificently.

ORANGE-APPLE PIE

Cook 6 apples (sliced) in ½ cup of orange juice, ½ cup of sugar and a dash of salt until tender.

Line pie plate with crust. Beat 1 egg white until it is frothy. Brush crust with egg white and sprinkle generously with brown sugar and several dashes of cinnamon. Place apple mixture in the shell, adding ⅓ to ½ cup more of sugar. Cut in ½ stick of butter. Cut pastry strips for top. Brush strips with remainder of egg white. Bake 30 minutes at 325 degrees on the bottom rack of your oven. Move to center and bake 30 minutes more.

From her husband's grandmother Frances has a recipe for apple cake which Jack calls "mountain crepe suzettes." It calls for thin, thin pancakes baked and topped with grated fresh apples (about 1½ cups for four servings). Cover the apple mixture generously with sugar and pour melted butter over all.

Ruby Chadwick makes a fresh apple pound cake which is something special in the way of pound cake.

RUBY'S FRESH APPLE POUND CAKE

1½ cups cooking oil
2 cups sugar
3 eggs

Combine and beat for three minutes at medium speed. Add 3 cups sifted flour, 1 teaspoon salt, 1 teaspoon soda and 2 teaspoons vanilla flavoring.

Fold in 3 large apples cut in small pieces and 1 cup chopped pecans.

Bake in a tube cake pan, which has been well greased and floured, for 1 hour and 20 minutes at 325 degrees. Cool 20 minutes and pour on a sauce made of the following:

1 stick butter, ½ cup light brown sugar (packed), 2 tablespoons milk. Bring to a boil and cook for twenty minutes. While hot pour on the cooled cake. It will be thin and will soak into the cake.

The custom of drying summer's apples for winter's use still prevails around Sweet Apple. In apple season nearly every household in the settlement has a rack of sliced apples drying in the sun. Ruby says one day of drying on a scrubbed sheet of tin is usually enough for thin-sliced apples. Then she seals them in jars and has them all winter for apple turnovers.

To make turnovers, says Ruby, cook the dried apples in a little water and sweeten to taste. She does not add spice to this mixture but spoons the plain sweet apples onto rounds of biscuit dough. (Canned biscuits rolled thin are handy for this but you can start from scratch if you want to.) Fold the dough into a half-moon, pinch the edges together and prick the sides with a fork (to avoid small apple explosions later). Fry the turnover in a little fat, one or two at a time, browning it on both sides. Sprinkle with sugar and serve up hot or cold. Ruby usually takes about two dozen of these to church dinners, sometimes varying it with peach turnovers which are made the same way.

Another use of dried apples is in an old-fashioned stacked cake, which Frances makes, using six thin layers and putting them together with spicy apple filling.

APPLE STACK CAKE

2 cups sugar
1 cup shortening
2 eggs
1 teaspoon baking soda
3 teaspoons baking powder
6 cups flour
1 teaspoon salt
½ cup buttermilk
2 teaspoons vanilla

Mix. Divide batter into 6 equal parts. Press into six 8-inch pans, greased and floured. Bake at 450 degrees for 10 minutes.

Filling

2 pounds dried apples, cooked and mashed
1¾ cups brown sugar
1 cup white sugar
4 teaspoons cinnamon
1 teaspoon cloves
1 teaspoon allspice

To the cooked and mashed apples add other ingredients and mix. Spread between layers and on top and sides. Let stand 12 hours before cutting.

After my first summer at Sweet Apple I gave up trying to can, preserve, pickle, jelly or jam everything that ripened on bush or tree. Apple jelly, for instance, was a hideous disappointment to me. It took hours to make, what with dripping the juice through a bag and measuring and stirring and all that. When it was done I thought it was lovely and far more *apple-y* tasting than the grocery store kind but guests, put to the blindfold test, couldn't tell the difference. Even when I tinted some of it pale green and flavored it with mint from the yard it wasn't singularly or spectacularly homemade tasting.

But there is one thing worth a bout with the preserving kettle and that's Olivia's apple relish. I had a terrible time getting the recipe because Olivia cooks by ear. I even spent a day with her, working along beside her and the dialogue went like this:

"How much vinegar do you use, Olivia?"

"Well, according to how much stuff you've got. I don't measure but you can judge."

"How much stuff? How many apples, for instance?"

"More apples than anything else. But not so many. Henry and Larry and I picked enough in just a few minutes."

"How many peppers?"

"Oh, say a peck. A peck more or less."

"How many green tomatoes? How many red peppers? How many onions?"

"You can kind of tell when you get started. Take a spoon and taste."

Even working along beside her it was difficult to get exact measurements but I have persevered and I think this is the recipe. If you come anywhere close to the flavor Olivia achieves it will be worth it.

OLIVIA'S APPLE RELISH

12 large apples
6 green bell peppers
6 red bell peppers
6 medium onions
12 large or 20 medium green tomatoes

Grind all these in food chopper and let drain or squeeze out the juice. Bring to a boil 4 cups sugar, 3 cups apple cider vinegar and add above mixture. Cook 15 or 20 minutes. Seal in clean jars. Makes 8 pints.

After the apple season passes I don't think much about desserts, with the possible exception of a blackberry cobbler, until a cool rainy day in the fall when it's pleasant to stay indoors and engage in such womanly pursuits as cookie or cake baking. Then I sometimes riffle through my little file of old recipes Muv has given me, more to read her footnotes, I think, than from serious interest in cooking.

Some of them are yellow and brittle, some written in pencil

so faint I can't read them. One such recipe is for Woodford Pudding and Muv has written at the top: "Miss Pearl Whittle gave me this. She married Aunt Puss Grimes' Ernie."

The principals are all strangers to me, people from Muv's girlhood, I suspect. But I tried the recipe out of curiosity and it turned out to be good.

WOODFORD PUDDING

3 eggs
1 cup sugar
1 cup flour
1 cup preserves (peaches best)
½ cup butter
1 teaspoon baking soda dissolved in 3 teaspoons sour milk
Bake slowly

Sauce

1 cup butter
1 cup cream
1 cup sugar
1 egg yolk

Let come to a simmer and flavor. Mrs. Ernie Grimes (nee Pearl Whittle) doesn't belabor the matter with directions but I muddled through, baking the pudding in a casserole and pouring the sauce over it.

At the top of another page there is in Muv's firm backhand script this note: "This is my old-time potato pone recipe. I've had it as far back as I can remember. Grandma made it often because she had more potatoes than anything else."

SWEET POTATO PONE

2½ cups raw grated sweet potatoes
1 cup molasses
2 eggs
2 cups milk ("I use 1 cup milk, 1 cup evaporated milk," Muv has written in.)
1 tablespoon melted shortening ("I use ½ stick margarine.")
1 teaspoon grated orange peel
1 tablespoon brown sugar
1 teaspoon powdered cinnamon

To the grated potatoes add molasses, well-beaten eggs, milk and shortening and orange peel. Turn into an iron skillet and bake about 45 minutes. At about the end of 25 minutes sprinkle the brown sugar and cinnamon over the top.

Also from Muv's grandmother is a recipe for butter roll. "We were all so fond of it when Grandma made it," Muv wrote at the top. "Lots of older folks still make it. A grand late-breakfast dish."

GREAT-GRANDMA'S BUTTER ROLL

Make a rich dough, like pie pastry. Roll out as for jelly roll, put dabs of sweet butter all over dough, sprinkle with sugar and nutmeg. Roll up and bake. Muv's note: "Delicious as is or with butter and cream sauce, slightly sweetened. Very good."

Many of Muv's recipes assume a prescience among the pots and pans that I don't have. They will be long on the recipe's origin and short on directions. Over a list of ingredients for coconut custard, Muv has written: "I don't suppose you remember Laura Broxson. She gave me this recipe when she taught on East Bay. She later married Judge Harvell's son."

I have never tried to make Laura Broxson's coconut custard but at least I know what goes in it and whose son she married.

Muv really enjoys making cakes more than anything else and for that reason her cake recipes are pretty complete and easy to follow. One oddly named "Tom Cake" carries this note: "This recipe has been in Charlie Adee's family for five generations."

I don't know Charlie but I'm glad his family handed down:

TOM CAKE

1 box seeded raisins
1 cup sugar
½ cup butter
2 eggs
2 cups flour
1 teaspoon each cinnamon, allspice, baking soda
1 teaspoon salt
Water drained from raisins after cooking

Cover raisins with water, bring to boil, let simmer 10 minutes. Set aside to cool while mixing cake batter. Cream butter, sugar and eggs well. Sift dry ingredients together. Drain water from raisins and mix, alternating with dry ingredients, into butter-sugar-egg mixture until all is used. Last add steamed raisins.

Bake in 12 × 12-inch cake pan at 375 degrees for about an hour or until cake springs back at touch. May be baked in loaf pan. Ice with standard butter-sugar icing. Add a teaspoon fresh lemon juice to the icing. Cut in squares and serve warm. Stays moist for days.

When there is a church supper or picnic in Alford Muv always knows whose cakes are made with butter and hand-beaten and who cheated and used a cake mix. When a cake is something special she quickly seeks out the cook and sets down the recipe.

Under one labeled "Mrs. Melvin's Sour Cream Cake," she wrote, "Food for the gods. She can't recall where she got the recipe."

It's also a light and flavorsome cake for mortals.

MRS. MELVIN'S SOUR CREAM CAKE

2 cups plain flour sifted three times with ½ teaspoon baking soda and ¼ teaspoon salt

3 cups sugar

½ pound butter

1 cup commercial sour cream

6 eggs separated, whites beaten stiff and added last

Beat egg yolks. Cream sugar and butter together, add egg yolks, gradually add flour mixture. Blend in stiffly beaten egg whites. Bake in tube pan at 350 degrees for 1 hour.

On a recipe for prune spice cake Muv has written, "This is a most delicious cake. Roxy served it with coffee at her house one afternoon (Nov. 26, 1950) and I just had to get the recipe."

Such a note persuades me and before I know it I'm looking for the sifter and the cake pans.

PRUNE SPICE CAKE

Wash about 2 cups prunes, cover with water, add small amount of sugar. Cook slowly about ½ hour. Beat together for 10 minutes 1 cup sugar, ½ teaspoon each nutmeg, cinnamon, cloves, and 2 whole eggs. Add alternately 1 cup whipped buttermilk, 1 teaspoon baking soda, 2 cups sifted flour, ½ teaspoon baking powder, ½ teaspoon salt, 1 cup very finely chopped cooked prunes, ½ cup melted butter. Pour mixture into two well-buttered 8-inch layer tins. Put into 300-degree oven and turn oven up to 350 degrees immediately to start baking on rising heat. Bake 25 to 30 minutes.

Fresh lemon-butter cream frosting: Mix 2 cups powdered sugar, ½ cup butter, adding juice of 1 lemon and a bit of grated lemon rind, if you wish. Fold in stiffly beaten white of 1 egg.

For a plain everyday cake Muv often stirs up a jelly cake and I have had moderate success following her recipe.

MUV'S JELLY CAKE

1 cup sugar
½ cup butter
3 eggs
½ cup sweet milk
2 cups flour
2 heaping teaspoons baking powder

Mix as any cake. Bake in 3 layers. When cool spread jelly between layers. Sprinkle top with powdered sugar.

Two of Muv's cakes I have never tried to bake are the lemon cheese and the fabulous Lane cake, which she brings us for Christmas and sometimes bakes for a birthday if the birthday person has had a hard year and needs something special and festive in his or her life. I don't think the recipes given here are particularly difficult but I have a perhaps superstitious fear of falling short of what Muv brings off with perfection.

LEMON CHEESE CAKE

- 1 cup butter
- 2 cups sugar
- 4 eggs
- 3 cups flour
- 3 teaspoons baking powder
- 1 cup milk
- 1 teaspoon vanilla

Cream sugar and butter and add beaten eggs. Fold in sifted dry ingredients alternately with the milk. Add vanilla. Bake in 3 layers at 350 degrees about 30 minutes.

Filling

2 lemons, juice and rind
3 egg yolks
½ cup butter
1 cup sugar

Combine ingredients and cook in double boiler until thickened. Cool and spread between layers.

The Lane cake recipe is an old one, named for a south Alabama family where it originated. The recipe calls for bourbon or brandy in the filling and although Muv's town is dry and her church and her immediate circle of friends frown on spirits in any form, she feels so strongly about the Lane cake that she will go to almost any length to get the proper seasoning for it. Once this resulted in a harrowing experience in a Panama City bistro. Muv rode down to the coast after church one day with one of her friends and while the friend was on another errand she slipped into the first place she saw with a neon sign blinking "Bar."

"It was a nice sunny day," Muv reported to us, "but dark as the inside of a cow in that place. I had on my good church clothes, hat and gloves and all, and this creature came slithering up to me wearing . . . I don't know what."

"Probably a cocktail dress, Muv," one of the children suggested.

"Maybe so," said Muv. "Anyway she looked half naked and she was downright impudent. She said, 'Madam, this is a cocktail lounge.' So I just drew myself up and said, 'My dear, I didn't *think* it was the Methodist parsonage! I'll have half a pint of Early Times please.'"

However the habitués of the bar may have felt about it, *we* thought the cake was well worth Muv's expedition.

LANE CAKE

8 egg whites
1 cup butter
1 teaspoon vanilla
2 cups sugar
3¼ cups flour
2 teaspoons baking powder
1 cup sweet milk

Cream butter and sugar until light. Add flour, baking powder and milk a little at the time. Add stiffly beaten egg whites and vanilla. Mix well and bake in 4 layers.

Filling

Beat well together 8 egg yolks, 1 cup sugar and ½ cup butter, stirring all the time. Add 1 cup raisins, 1 cup chopped pecans, a wine glass of bourbon or brandy and 1 teaspoon vanilla. Spread between layers, sprinkle top with freshly grated coconut, add candied cherries for decoration. Store a few days before serving.

Muv's pound cake is another Christmas specialty, which I wouldn't try to copy on just any day, but consider well worth an Occasion.

POUND CAKE

1 pound butter
1 pound sugar
10 eggs
1 pound flour
½ teaspoon mace
2 tablespoons brandy flavoring

Cream butter, add sugar and beat. Separate egg yolks and whites. Beat egg yolks until thick. Add to butter and sugar. Sift and add dry ingredients. Fold in egg whites and add flavoring. Bake in a tube pan in a slow oven, 325 degrees, until done. Let cool in pan for 15 or 20 minutes before turning out on rack.

Maude Miles has from a former neighbor, Mrs. John Foster, a somewhat smaller pound cake, which comes out crusty and brown, born, says Maude, to go with a freezer of homemade ice cream.

FOSTER-MILES POUND CAKE

Cream ½ pound of butter and 1¾ cups of sifted sugar. Add 5 eggs and 2 cups of sifted flour, 1 egg at a time and one-fifth of the flour at a time. Beat 5 minutes for each addition at low speed. Add ¼ teaspoon lemon extract and ¼ teaspoon vanilla. Bake in greased tube pan at 275 degrees for 1 hour and 25 minutes—sometimes longer.

Another old-fashioned country cake which can be iced or served plain is Maude's

HOT MILK CAKE

4 eggs
2 cups white sugar
2 teaspoons baking powder
2 cups cake flour
1 teaspoon vanilla
1 scant teaspoon lemon extract
¼ pound butter
1 cup sweet milk

Beat eggs until real light. Mix sugar in eggs. Sift baking powder in flour. Then mix flour in sugar and eggs. Put milk and butter in saucepan, bring to boil. Pour over other ingredients. Add flavoring and mix. Bake three layers or in a loaf or tube pan. If the latter, it should take about 1 hour.

In this day of easy-to-buy frozen and packaged cookies I seldom think of baking them except when I long for the old-fashioned tea cakes, which have to be homemade. The tea cakes of my childhood were big and soft and marvelously filling. I did not know the word "cookie" until I was a big child and heard a neighbor from Pennsylvania use it. All little cakes were tea cakes to us.

The recipe which comes closest to producing tea cakes as I remember them is written in Muv's handwriting with this note: "This is Aunt Mollie's tea cake recipe."

AUNT MOLLIE'S TEA CAKES

1 cup sugar
1 egg
½ cup butter, melted
¼ cup buttermilk
1 teaspoon baking soda
1 teaspoon vanilla
3½ cups plain flour

Beat egg, add sugar and butter barely melted. Mix soda with buttermilk and add to mixture. Add vanilla and work in flour, just enough to handle. Roll dough lightly and cut cookies with baking powder can or water glass. Beneath that Muv added: "You can say cookie cutter. Aunt Mollie didn't have one."

Ginger cakes are also hard to duplicate at the store. The crisp gingersnaps are something entirely different from the big soft ginger cakes of yore. Mrs. Lum Crow makes these often for her children and grandchildren. (Mrs. Crow is called Dessie by Mr. Crow and their contemporaries and I found out by accident that her real name is the beautiful Odessa. Mr. Crow took me to Ebenezer Church graveyard to see the fine joint "tomb rock" he bought several years back and had inscribed with their names and birth dates "so the young 'uns won't have to bother when we're gone." There, gravestone proper, was the name Odessa.)

MRS. CROW'S GINGER CAKES

1 cup sugar
1 cup syrup
1 cup butter

Heat together and add gradually to flour into which you have sifted 1 teaspoon baking soda, ½ teaspoon salt and 1 tablespoon ginger, working it in with 1 cup sweet milk. Mrs. Crow makes up her cookies in the old wooden dough tray which is always half full of flour and ready for her to make biscuits. She has no idea how much flour her ginger

cakes take. Enough, she says, to make a soft dough.
I started with 3 cups and it's about right.

One other cookie that I think is abundantly worth the trouble and cannot be duplicated at the store is:

MAUDE'S FUDGE CAKES

Cream ½ cup butter, 1 cup brown sugar. Add 1 unbeaten egg and 2 squares of unsweetened chocolate melted. Add ½ cup sweet milk, into which ½ teaspoon baking soda has been dissolved. Then add 1 cup stoned, halved dates, 1 cup black walnut meats coarsely chopped, 2 cups flour.

Drop by tablespoonfuls on a greased cookie sheet, holding in reserve 1 tablespoonful of batter to add to the icing. Bake in a moderate oven—and watch, says Maude.

Icing

Melt 2 squares of chocolate and add to 1 cup of milk, along with 2 cups of sugar and the aforementioned tablespoonful of batter. Cook until it forms a soft ball. Do not stir after it starts to boil. Add 2 tablespoons of butter and cool. Add 1 teaspoon vanilla and beat. (Not much beating will be required because the icing needs to be soft to spread on the cookies. If it gets too stiff to spread you can thin it with a little hot milk.)

Mrs. Rossie Hancock, whose family were old settlers in our community, gave Maude Miles her recipe for Christmas custard. It is a thin boiled custard which may be eaten with a spoon and serves equally well as a base for eggnog. Mrs. Hancock made it in hefty amounts to feed legions of Christmas company.

Maude reduced the amounts to a more moderate size and the recipe is worth the effort of departing from ready mixes because of its texture and the subtle flavoring of orange achieved by simmering half an orange in the custard for a few minutes.

CHRISTMAS CUSTARD

1 quart milk
2 egg yolks
2 egg whites
½ cup sugar
Pinch salt
⅛ cup cornstarch
1 orange

Scald milk. Beat egg yolks and before the milk begins to boil add eggs slowly, stirring rapidly. Mix cornstarch with a little milk and add, also salt and the juice of the orange. Put half the orange, pulp, rind and all, into the pan and simmer for a few minutes. Remove orange rind and add sugar. When the custard coats a spoon remove from the fire and add stiffly beaten egg whites.

Another old-fashioned custard recipe is from the Tabor archives. It goes in a baked pie crust and is called:

TRANSPARENT CUSTARD

4 egg yolks
1 whole egg
1 goose egg of butter (Frances and I estimate that is about a stick, having no goose eggs for comparison.)
1 cup sugar
1 cup sweet milk

> Combine ingredients and simmer over hot water until thick and pour into pie crust. Beat 4 egg whites into a meringue and top the custard. Brown in oven.

The recipe books I have that I have enjoyed the most always end with some general household hints or rules for the proper conduct of a home. Jettie Bell Johnson's old book, for instance, admonishes the young homemaker that "to leave the soap in the bottom of the scrubbing pail, the Sapolio in the basin of water and to spatter the black lead or stove polish on the floor are wasteful, slatternly habits."

The Herters in their "Bull Cook" collection end with directions on how to survive in the wilderness in the event of a hydrogen bomb attack.

Marjorie Kinnan Rawlings, bless her, simply reminds cooks that the spirit in which food is prepared is the most important quality about it. "Carefully . . . willingly . . . imaginatively," she says, with those who eat—family, friends or strangers— conscious of their welcome.

"The breaking together of bread, the sharing of salt, is too ancient a symbol of friendliness to be profaned," she says, concluding with the reminder from Proverbs: "Better is a dinner of herbs where love is."

I have my own list of rules for surviving in a house without being swamped by a lot of details that don't interest me much at the time. There are, of course, times when every woman can tackle an all-out, stomp-down, earth-moving house cleaning with joy and verve. But there are times when you'd rather take a walk or read a book, dig in the garden or take a nap than be turning out closets or polishing silver or dusting behind things. I mentioned this to a friend and she said, "What would Muv say to such talk?" I was able to assure her triumphantly that all I know about not letting housework get the upper hand I learned from my sainted mother.

"We come," Muv told me once, "from a long line of indifferent housekeepers."

She cited her aunts, Aunt Babe, Aunt Mollie and Aunt Dilly, who helped to rear her and always had time to go fishing or play the fiddle and dance or whip up a cake and throw an impromptu party. The house where they all lived together in their later years seemed clean and orderly to me, if I thought about it at all, and they were always ready for a picnic, a trip or any kind of junket that came up.

Muv herself has ever had fantastic energy and I've come home from school many times to find that she had pulled our maid of all work, Cooter, out of the house and both of them were building a rose arbor or painting the house. To manage time for things you want to do and still avert being divorced by your husband as an absolute slattern is simple by Muv's rules.

The first thing is to make your bed, if you have time. If you don't, strip the covers off it and air it. This is neater looking and would make any random observer think you are not lazy but simply big on fresh air.

Two, always hang up clothes. It's better for clothes and you can find them easier if the house catches on fire.

Three, never—repeat *never*—leave dirty dishes on the table or in the sink. If you haven't the time or inclination to wash them, hide them. A sink full of dirty dishes soaking in greasy water advertises to the world that you are a sloven. It's just as quick and easy to stack them neatly in a pan and stick them in the oven or cover them with a spanky clean dish towel until you get around to washing them. (Of course the advent of the electric dishwasher in my life was right in line with my home training. It offers the perfect hiding place for dishes. But once I hid a panful of dishes so thoroughly it took me three days to find them.)

These are rudimentary—a neat bed, a shining sink. Muv's other rules are, I suppose, window dressing. A house needs fresh flowers if you can get them, growing plants anyhow. If the weather is cool there should be either a fire burning on the hearth or one laid and ready to light, fruit at hand to eat and something to read. With these things a little dust here and there on table tops and chair rungs hardly seems important.

To have the table set and something fragrant cooking, even if it's going to be hours before it's ready, gives a home-coming man or child a feeling of welcome and well-being. My friend

Margaret Castleberry pursued this line of thought in advice to all young brides. Before a husband comes home, she said, no matter what you're planning to cook, fry up a few onions. "They smell so good and *promising!*"

One last bit of household lore that has served me in good stead at Sweet Apple came from my friend Angeline Levey, who once had a maid who was neat, efficient and industrious but absolutely adamant about not "working over my head" or washing windows. She said she had never done either and she didn't intend to.

"But what do you do in your own house when the windows get dirty?" Angie asked.

"Mrs. Levey," said the maid, "if they be's so dirty I can't see out the window, I looks out the door."

Winter, 1985

Change has come to Sweet Apple settlement. Some of it is sad, as change often is. We have lost many of the people whose help and friendship made making a home in the old log cabin both possible and pleasurable. A dozen or more have died; some have moved away.

A few years ago little Merthiolate-colored flags showed up on stakes in what we had come to regard as "our" woods, heralding the approach of suburbia. Now paved streets, with electric lights at the corners and city water plugs marching alongside, crisscross the old pastures and fields and pierce the wooded hills. Splendid stone chalets, Victorian mansions and English manor houses have risen on the slopes and in the hollows.

Where I once gathered wild persimmons and blackberries, newcomers have put in swimming pools and tennis courts. Where we once heard Denver Cox gee-hawing his mule as he plowed a cornfield, we now hear hammer blows, power saws and bulldozers clearing sites for still more building. Many of the cherished landmarks are gone. The secret woodland spots we regarded as our own private hideaways — lichened rocks beside little creeks, a secluded mossy bank curtained by muscadine vines, a pine thicket where the pipsissewa grew — are now open and owned, the property of newcomers who, in all probability, love them too, and may show it by having them *landscaped*.

Sweet Apple cabin itself has resisted change but not

completely. We added another cabin in the early 1970's, buying one our neighbor Ralph Dangar found three miles down the road near old New Home church. It was the same size and the same age as Sweet Apple cabin, except its logs were square cut instead of halved. Our friend Quinton Johnson chalked numbers on the logs, dismantled the cabin and hauled it piece by piece to a spot down the hill from the house. The rains came and washed off the numbers, but eventually we got the old house on its feet on rock pillars and connected it to the original cabin by a breezeway. It gives us bed space for more grandchildren, who have also multiplied with the passage of the years.

The road to Chadwick's store, which has ever gone past Sweet Apple cabin, is still blessedly free of concrete, but road crews from the public works camp are more meticulous nowadays about keeping it smooth and passable. There's a lot of traffic now, including two new services — the school bus and the rural mail carrier. We formerly met both in all weathers down at the crossroads.

Wistful as I sometimes get for the neighbors who are gone and the way of life which may be no longer country any day now, I have to rejoice in some changes. Our pipes still freeze, our furnance still expires, cars turn temperamental and refuse to move. But when that happens, we turn to the finest modern convenience of all — our closest new neighbors, Jim and Nan Warren, who moved to the woods next to us a few years ago.

Index